WALTER DE LA MARE
A Study of his Poetry

Walter de la Mare
A Study of his Poetry

BY HENRY CHARLES DUFFIN

Select Bibliographies Reprint Series

 BOOKS FOR LIBRARIES PRESS
FREEPORT, NEW YORK

STANDARD BOOK NUMBER:

8369-5043-7

LIBRARY OF CONGRESS CATALOG CARD NUMBER:

71-94269

PRINTED IN THE UNITED STATES OF AMERICA

CONTENTS

THE PORTRAITS

No. 1 (frontispiece) from a photograph by Hoppé taken about 1912.

No. 2 (facing page 165) from a photograph by John Gay taken in 1948.

TO WALTER DE LA MARE

My dear W.J.,

My hope has been to make this a lovely book on a lovely theme, but the one indisputably lovely thing about it is that it brought us together. When, so many years ago, I sent you the first inadequate draft, you met the situation by mislaying the typescript, but you asked me to come and see you at Taplow, and what the friendship which grew out of that meeting has meant to me and my wife only her ardent and uninhibited tongue could fittingly express. You for your part have learnt the esoteric joy of sandwiches for tea.

On the whole I share that critical opinion which says that appreciation of an artist's work is only hindered by a close knowledge of his life, and I believe it to be equally true that a poet's personality does not often stand up to a comparison with his poetry. But if Dorothy and I had to choose between you and your poetry: never (as Carlyle phrased a similar dilemma—now resolved!)—never to have had the poems, or never to have known W.J.: it were a grave, an agonizing question. Fortunately the problem does not arise: you we have while life and memory endure, and we and the world have your poems until mankind forgets the meaning of poetry.

So I come to my immediate purpose, which is to thank you for your permission to inscribe this book to you. I do so with extraordinary pleasure, and have the happiness to write myself,

With affection and admiration,
Always yours,
H.C.D.

HOVE, 1949

PRELIMINARY

B E T W E E N the inception of this book and the writing of its last word many years have passed. It originated in a white-hot enthusiasm for its subject, but a World War and other more relevant interruptions have provided ample time for the cooling of that enthusiasm. Time there has been, but no cooling. More than once in these last years I have read over again the bulk of de la Mare's poetry, and have found there an almost unparalleled beauty and wonder, mystery, revelation and assuagement of soul beyond anything that can be got except from the greatest of poets and musicians. Such poetry, producing its effect moreover with such beautiful lucidity, may seem not to require—not perhaps even able to bear— a commentary. Certainly nothing but the poems themselves will convey the poet's full intention. That is why I have sometimes in the course of my exposition made use of de la Mare's own words and phrases to a degree verging on the impermissible.

When I wrote about Hardy's novels without regard to his poetry I was very properly taken to task (and atoned as far as might be for my sins in later editions). I think it will be unreasonable if objection is brought against my treating de la Mare's poetry in isolation. He is a supreme poet: his utterly delightful prose stories represent surplus creative energy; their light is of the same kind, but it is a reflected light, like that which makes the moon the modest partner of the sun. And not quite the same kind of light either. As a

poet de la Mare is essentially a visionary: in prose he
walks on earth, though in byways unknown to most
of us. His prose imagination dwells just under the
threshold of the world we live in; his poetry speaks
from worlds infinitely afar. His poems are the product
of the mystic dream: his stories come out of an
impish inquisitiveness, a humorous and unhallowed
speculation on the order of the universe. He moves
through the human comedy like a good-natured and
intelligent poltergeist. He goes about with spade and
pick-axe digging up the queer side of things.

De la Mare has been for over forty years a lyric
poet, and I am not disposed to believe that in 1946 he
turned philosopher with *The Traveller*. This longest
of his poems is an enchanting tale, written throughout
with great lyrical beauty, and any didactic intention
there may be is entirely and rightly subordinated to
the narrative zest and the vesture of lovely words. I
like best to read the poem as an elaboration of one of
de la Mare's own dreams, or, better still, as another
self-portrait, a rendering of his own "unbroken
pilgrimage", the "sum of all his communings" with
the unseen. As he begins—"This Traveller broke
at length" out of gloom to look on beauty, is it not of
himself that he speaks? Is it not his own gasp of wonder that we hear? When the horseman sits dreaming
about himself as a child gazing entranced at the "lunar
landscape", can we fail to recognize our poet, or to be
aware of who it is that wonders if he be man or ghost?
I hardly dare to suggest that the ivory mare, so
greatly beloved and so intimately joined with her
master, is the poet's muse, and a pun on his own name

—a name which is for many of us identified with the
very idea of poetry.

I cannot hope to find universal approval for my
(perhaps laboured) distinction between Reality and
Truth, but I can at least adduce support from the
right quarter. In de la Mare's introduction to his
anthology of *Love* it is written, "the elect fall in love
with Truth, the imaginative with Reality". As for
my division of the poetry under these two terms, this
may excite positive antagonism, especially as—
though doing my best to hold the balance even—I
have not only been unable quite to conceal my personal attachment for "reality", but have found "the
"the poetry of reality" to bulk largely in the early
volumes, as published. Dr. Strachan praises *The Veil*
(and by implication the two succeeding volumes, *The
Fleeting* and *Memory*) for its "courageous type of
beauty" achieved in "uglier material". Forrest Reid,
with like reference, calls de la Mare's "last poetry . . .
infinitely deeper than the first". Mr. Edward Davison
has expressed regret that he should be chiefly known
by his "lighter books". It will be obvious that my
point of view is different, but what I am anxious to do
here is to ask that when I have found it necessary to
speak of the "earlier" or the "later" poetry those
terms shall be taken as referring to form and content
rather than to chronology, even though it is a fact that
most of the "poetry of reality" appeared before 1920
and most of the "poetry of truth" after that date. In
the *Collected Poems* and *Collected Rhymes and Verses* of
1942 and 1944 the contents of the original volumes
were shaken up like the coloured fragments in a

kaleidoscope. The new arrangement recreates the poetry, but I cannot imagine lovers of de la Mare ceasing to cherish for their own sweet sakes such integral and individual books as *The Listeners, Motley and Peacock Pie*.

A word about duplicate titles. It is well known that in a number of instances de la Mare has given the same name to two or more poems. In referring to these poems I have distinguished them by appending the letters (a), (b), etc. A glance at the following list (which gives the first words of each poem and the volume or volumes in which it is to be found) will then show exactly which poem is in question.

C.P. = *Collected Poems* 1942; C.R. = *Collected Rhymes and Verses* 1944; S.C. = *Songs of Childhood*; P.1906 = *Poems* 1906; P.P. = *Peacock Pie*; L. = *The Listeners*; Mot. = *Motley*; V. = *The Veil*; F. = *The Fleeting*; Mem. = *Memory*; B-G. = *The Burning-glass*.

Alone (a) A very old woman. C.P. and L.
Alone (b) The abode of the nightingale. C.P. and Mot.
Ariel (a) This lad when a child. C.P. and F.
Ariel (b) Ariel! Ariel! B-G.
The Blind Boy (a) I have no master. C.P. and Mot.
The Blind Boy (b) A spider her silken gossamer. B-G.
The Cage (a) Why did you flutter? C.P. and Mot.
The Cage (b) Thou angel face! C.P. and Mem.
The Dreamer (a) O thou who giving helm and sword. C.P. and Mot.
The Dreamer (b) The woods were still. C.P. and Mem.
Dreams (a) Be gentle O hands of a child. C.P. and L.
Dreams (b) Even one who long hath travelled. C.P. and F.
Evening (a) When twilight darkens. C.P. and P.1906.

Preliminary

Evening (b) The little cirque horizon wide. C.P. and Mem.

The Ghost (a) Peace in thy hands. C.P. and L.

The Ghost (b) Who knocks? C.P. and Mot.

Memory (a) When summer heat. C.P. and F.

Memory (b) Ah, memory thou strange deceit. C.P. and Mem.

Music (a) When music sounds. C.P. and Mot.

Music (b) O restless fingers. C.P. and V.

The Owl (a) What if to edge of dream. C.P. and V.

The Owl (b) The door-bell jangled. C.P. and F.

The Owl (c) Owl of the wildwood I. B-G.

Night (a) All from the light. C.P. and P.1906.

Night (b) That shining moon. C.P. and Mem.

The Phantom (a) Upstairs in the large closet, child. C.R. and S.C.

The Phantom (b) Wilt thou never come again. C.P. and P.1906.

A Portrait (a) A solemn plainfaced child. C.P. and Mem.

A Portrait (b) Old yet unchanged. B-G.

The Rainbow (a) I saw the lovely arch. C.R. and S.C.

The Rainbow (b) Stood twice ten-thousand warriors. B-G.

The Scarecrow (a) All winter through. C.P. and L.

The Scarecrow (b) In the abandoned orchard. B-G.

Shadow (a) Even the beauty of the rose. C.P. and P.1906.

Shadow (b) Beware! C.P. and Mem.

The Sleeper (a) As Ann came in. C.P. and L.

The Sleeper (b) The lovely sleeping. C.P. and F.

Snow (a) No breath of wind. C.R. and Poems 1919—34.

Snow (b) This meal-white snow. C.P. and Mem.

Solitude (a) Ghosts there must be with me. C.P.

Solitude (b) Wish and it's thine. C.R. and *Bells and Grass.*

The Stranger (a) In a nook of the wood. C.R.

The Stranger (b) A little after twilight. C.R. and *Bells and Grass.*

xiii

Preliminary

The Stranger (c) Half-hidden in a graveyard. C.P. and L.

The Stranger (d) In the woods as I did walk. C.P. and Mot.

The Tryst (a) Flee into some forgotten night. C.P. and Mot.

The Tryst (b) Faint now the colours. C.P. and F.

The Window (a) Behind the blinds. C.R. and P.P.

The Window (b) Sunlit, the lashes fringe. C.P. and Mem.

ACKNOWLEDGEMENT

My personal debt to Mr. de la Mare is beyond assessment or expression; all I can do here is to acknowledge his kindness in permitting me to quote extensively from his works in verse and prose, and letting me use the two hitherto unpublished photographs.

Acknowledgement is also due to Messrs. Faber & Faber, publishers of Mr. de la Mare's poetry.

PART I
THE POETRY OF REALITY

CHAPTER I

The Poetic Approach to Reality

D E LA MARE's aching sense of exile, expressed
in poem after passionate poem, is not peculiar
to him, or indeed to the poets. It is a mood of
the search for reality in which most thinking men are
intermittently engaged. Not continuously engaged,
of course: for one thing, our physical life draws its
sustenance from the unreal world of which it is a part;
for another, the world of appearance is desperately
interesting, and we could be well content to surrender
ourselves to its intricate and painful delights, were it
not that, once we have had "sight of that immortal
sea", we can never again be quite free of "obstinate
questionings". Life comes in time to be chiefly valued
for the glimpses and signs it affords of the greater
reality that life so imperfectly foreshadows. Those indeed who have not been vouchsafed the gleam ask
why it should be supposed that there is any further
reality behind appearance: kick a stone, break your
wrist, lose your job—there is nothing unreal about
these things. To say this means only that the events
named have a noticeable effect upon the senses or
upon the activities which make up the outward semblance of life. But (though the senses are perhaps
more trustworthy than has sometimes been suggested
by philosophers) the contemplation of the greater
part of human activity convinces of its hollow
unreality: it has no purpose other than to serve the

moment, it fits into no acceptable scheme. All the world of "business", and most of the world of politics, and half the world of industry and pleasure—what can these things be but phantasmagoria? They mean nothing—they shrink from the idea of permanence—the touch of eternity effaces them. And yet there can be no thought that life itself is unreal: for those who have the full sense of life there is no doubt that life as it appears to us rests on—or is a cross-section of—a reality which breaks through to one man here, to another man there. Bradley found reality in religious experience; Mr. Charles Morgan finds it in "art, love and death", de la Mare in dream—the dream of wake or sleep, intuitive understanding, contemplative union with the eternal. In general, reality is to be found in intense spiritual activity, and in its products: in religious experience, and the mystical knowledge that it brings; in nature worship (a kind of religious experience), and the vision of the world which it inspires; in the insight of genius, and its results in art; in love, and the happiness which is its outward visible form; in certain tenuous, ethereal contacts made by the mind in conditions of semi- or hyper-consciousness, and the direct apprehension thus obtained of spiritual reality. Modern physicists, and writers like Mr. J. W. Dunne and Mr. J. B. Priestley, have suggested that by experimenting with time we may achieve a technique of reality—in a million years or so.

Meanwhile we must be content with such fractional hints of reality as may come our way, and make the most of the richer contacts afforded us at one remove by the poets and musicians. It is the function of poetry to keep us in touch with the world of spirit of which the material world is an expression. It is only lyric poetry that does thus keep touch, and poetry that uses lyric as a medium. Hence the greatest kinds of poetry, dramatic and epic, are those which, while basing their themes on the life and actions of men, explore the world of spirit by virtue of their lyric afflatus. Lyric itself flies wholly in the spirit world; the lesser kinds, narrative, descriptive, didactic, are earth-bound.

The supreme importance of ultra-phenomenal reality, and the part played by aesthetic experience in leading us to it, are somewhat neglected in literary criticism. But there is something exceptionally obtuse about two reflections one occasionally hears passed upon de la Mare: "not, of course, a profound thinker"; and "essentially a children's poet, don't you feel?" Profound thinking is (doubtless!) a fascinating exercise, but its relation to poetry is not a necessary one. A poet may provide us with solutions to the problems of life, but if he does so it is as moralist or philosopher, not as poet. The poet's thinking, like our own, goes on within "the warm precincts of the cheerful day", but some part of his mind goes feeling out into the dark. He arrives at strange knowledge, but not by thinking. However "profound" your thought-processes, you cannot think your way through to reality: the requisite premisses are lacking.

As for the other criticism, it has more apparent relevance, but is wrong both in what it asserts and in what it implies. De la Mare is not, to any large extent, a children's poet, except in the way that *The Tempest* is a play for children. In the two-volume Collected Edition of 1942 and 1944, one volume is called *Collected Rhymes and Verses*, and it comprises the contents of those separate volumes which, de la Mare says, "were intended for children". Yet three out of four even of these "rhymes and verses" are poems in a fully adult sense: giving delight to children, indeed, just as *The Tempest* does, but moving the sensitive and experienced reader to tears, to dream, to an understanding of life and of what lies behind life. And still it remains true that not only in these poems but in the confessedly more serious productions of the companion volume, *Collected Poems*, de la Mare writes "as a child", in the sense of that wisest of all wise sayings, that which declares that to enter the Kingdom of God a man must "become as a child". The mind at work behind de la Mare's poetry has, for its creative qualities, just those which Jesus must have intended to be covered by His phrase: first, simplicity; then, humility, faith and love; clear-eyed wonder; fresh, direct, untroubled vision, unobscured by sin or doubt, free from the long years' accumulation of inhibition and reservation; complete surrender to the light of coming knowledge—delighted acceptance of miracle. Outside his study, too, in his normal human responses to life, de la Mare exhibits a preference for irrational explanations of phenomena which disconcerts the more commonplace mind of his interlocutor. Hermann Keyserling, who had some claim to be considered a "profound thinker", suggested that "the

6

non-rational faculties of the soul will in the future contribute most to progress".

Lyric poetry is the voice of God. But the voice speaks, in different poets, with varying degrees of authenticity. The degree of authenticity corresponds not so much with the greatness of the poet (greatness depends on many factors beside this one) as with the nature of the contact the poet is able to make with the underlying reality, with the spiritual beauty and truth which are the tangible substance of reality. De la Mare belongs to a very small band of poets whose contact is peculiarly close and vital because it partakes of the directness, the immediacy, of mysticism. In very many of his poems, constituting probably more than half of his total output, de la Mare makes us aware of a life, a world, an experience, which are instantly recognized as not only different from anything the common day has to offer, but more real, partaking more of the eternal, in the same way as the mystic's knowledge of God.* And it is especially to be noted that de la Mare not only communicates to us the fact that he has had this mystical (or, if you like, quasi-mystical) experience, but enables us to enter

* In his very valuable "preface to poetics", *Poetry and Contemplation*, Mr. G. Rostrevor Hamilton asserts his willingness to believe that the poetic experience is "significant of a wider reality", and admits that certain poems seem to "open the mind to a reality beyond itself"; but he declares that the concern of the critic, as distinct from the philosopher, is with poetry as an aesthetic experience alone. Nevertheless, to "the state of mind proper to the aesthetic attitude at a well-developed stage" he gives "the honourable name, 'contemplation' ", by which I suppose him to mean mystical understanding.

7

upon it (or something parallel to it) ourselves: this
he does through his supreme gift of poetic form,
which promotes in the mind an awareness by which
it participates in the poet's comprehension of the
uttermost nature of things.

The power of lyric form to carry the supreme poetic
message is of peculiar interest to English readers. For
English poetry means lyric poetry. Of all the factors
which go to make up Shakespeare's supremacy his
supreme lyric gift stands first.* Mr. Hilaire Belloc
has said that all great English poets are great in proportion as they are lyrical, and though the generaliza-
tion does not cover Pope, Dryden, Browning and
Hardy, it is in essence correct. Mr. Belloc attributes
our greatness in lyric to "the intensity of the English
imagination—visual imagination". I should go far-
ther than this, and regard English lyric as the prin-
cipal product of English mysticism (and indeed visual
imagination is an important item in the mystic equipment). Mysticism in its religious aspect has found
English soil less encouraging than that of some other
countries; what there is of it in English thought is
seen as clearly in our poetry, from Donne to Francis
Thompson, from Blake to AE and Evelyn Underhill,
as anywhere. But philosophic mysticism, and individual and personal mysticism, are much more con-

* This judgment has been questioned. But while we measure and
criticize Shakespeare's dramatic art we are silent before his absolute
power over words, the power to move the soul, by metrical speech,
to unknown joy and participation in the infinite. For every miracle
of characterization or situation there are twenty miracles of sheer
poetry. *Twelfth Night, Lear, The Tempest* are even greater as poems
than they are as plays.

8

genial to the English mind, and they are continuously present in the English lyric tradition. For the lyric ecstasy is one of the means to that immediacy of knowledge which is the aim of the mystic. How often we realize, in reading the English poets, that what we are made to *feel* by the poet's verses is, though dark and inexpressible, more than what we are made to *think*.

He is made one with Nature: there is heard
His voice in all her music. . . .

magic casements opening on the foam
Of perilous seas in faery lands forlorn.

To-morrow, and to-morrow, and to-morrow,
Creeps in this petty pace from day to day
To the last syllable of recorded time. . . .

Come, thou mortal wretch,
With thy sharp teeth this knot intrinsicate
Of life at once untie: poor venomous fool,
Be angry, and dispatch.

I tax not you, you elements, with unkindness;
I never gave you kingdom, called you children. . . .

Our revels now are ended. These our actors,
As I foretold you, were all spirits, and
Are melted into air. . . .

There sometimes doth a leaping fish
Send through the tarn a lonely cheer.

9

The silence that is in the starry sky,
The sleep that is among the lonely hills.

    the meadow your walks have left so sweet
That whenever a March wind sighs
He sets the jewel-print of your feet
In violets blue as your eyes.

When music sounds all that I was I am
Ere to this haunt of brooding dust I came. . . .

In some of these examples the over-effect, the sense of ulterior significance, is brought about by sheer force of words, sometimes by the strangeness of the thought; most often it is by the moving power of rhythmic form that we feel we have been put into touch with that immediate knowledge of reality which the poet achieved through the lyric ecstasy, and of which the detailed sense of the poem, conveyed in the words, is but a distant parallel, a faint shadow, an imperfect manifestation. The larger truth, the profounder experience, the infinitely more important knowledge, are not to be expressed in words as symbols of meaning. Meaning must be there, of course, but it must be dissolved on form. We come nearest to identifying ourselves with the poet and his otherwise incommunicable secret if we surrender our minds to the rhythmic form of his poem.*

Even meaning must often be disguised. Mystic knowledge, like other forms of esoteric truth, travels incognito—it has no name that we could understand:

* cf. Goethe: "There is something magical in rhythm; it even makes us believe that the sublime lies within our reach".

Jesus was compelled to present the Kingdom of Heaven in the likeness of a grain of mustard-seed. And so, when de la Mare speaks of Arabia and its music; of Martha's hazel-glen in the hush of an age gone by; of the quiet steeps of dreamland or the lonely dreams of a child; of the unchangeable that contrasts with earth's transiency; of the dark château and the house that was named Alas; of the sunken garden and the listening house, the tranquil hills and the coloured country of the Traveller; of the house of shadows and the kingdom of the Mad Prince and the steep of time whence the Knight of Finis charged with his challenge into space; of Nothing with its changeless vague of peace; of two gardens for two children in one mind; of a bird that taps at a window: when such themes as these fill up the lovely line of de la Mare we know he is remembering and trying to tell us about that deeper reality, incredibly strange and strangely momentous, of his experience; then we must lean our ear and hearken for the rhythm that is to lift us into the mental state in which alone we too can enter upon that experience.

Remembering and—trying to tell us? There appears to be some doubt about this. De la Mare himself has been known to deny that it is the poet's business to "communicate" his vision to his readers: in so far as "communication" enters into the question at all it goes on only between the poet and himself. There is force in the contention: the poet is no public orator: if there is an activity which is entirely private, poetry is that activity. Yet de la Mare has also written (in his short story, *The Green Room*), "Poetry, good or bad,

11

depends for its very life on the hospitable reader, as tinder awaits the spark". Surely this is true. A poem is the experience of a poet expressed in poetic form and read by a reader to whom the poetic form communicates the poet's experience.* Not only is it incomplete without the second part of the operation; it is, as de la Mare says, non-existent, dead. Poetry, like beauty, exists only in and by the presence of an appreciative mind. Certainly the poet's own mind may supply the appreciation: and it is one of the marvels of the human mind that it can not only create but provide the response to its own creation (this is as good an argument for immortality as Mr. Dunne's infinite recessions). But until some other sensitive mind has responded the poet cannot know whether his response is a true one. His responses—of pleasure, of emotion, of transport —will be the same whether the poem is good or bad, provided it is the best he is capable of. His response to his "creation" must be strongly affected by his knowledge of its origin, and only when a second person, with spiritual equipment not too diverse, comes along and exhibits the same kind and degree of response as his own can the poet know that he has performed a genuine act of creation. The poet's purpose may be to lay up beauty and wonder in his own heart,

* When Mr. G. R. Hamilton (*Poetry and Contemplation*, p. 107) says the work of a poet is to create poetic experience, not communicate it, he means that the original experience of the poet— something in his "everyday" life which made him want to write a poem—has not to be communicated. But when this experience has been "created" by being put into poetic form, it must be capable of being taken over by another mind, and what is this but communication?

12

but the outward, perhaps secondary, result of his doing so must be the carrying of beauty and wonder into our hearts too.

And especially wonder. De la Mare has named among the springs of poetry "a sense of wonder and mystery", "a hope and hunger for the unknown". The world that we know and half-understand is so wonderful that a man might lose all his days musing on its perpetual miracle. But the eternal world of which we see only a shadow, and that only in favoured moments; which we know, if at all, only by inference: this we guess is wonderful beyond our dreams. And the poet's true business is not to lead us to truth, nor, primarily, even to bring us beauty or joy, but to make us aware and keep us reminded of the unimaginable wonder of life, of the unknown, of reality—the reality which is ultimately God.

CHAPTER II

The Approach by Form

IN spite of its somewhat contemptuous dismissal by Croce in the *Aesthetic*, Walter Pater's description of music as "the ideal of all art, because in music substance is indistinguishable from form", maintains its value as a criterion. The soul of any work of art, as A. C. Bradley showed twenty years before Croce, doubtless lies neither in its form nor in its content, but in the relation of the two. Nevertheless, in music the form element of the synthesis is immeasurably the more important, while, at the other end of the scale, in a piece of didactic verse form may be negligible. Hence it seems not unreasonable to suggest a gradation of poetry in accordance with the ratio of the form-content relation. If this were done, it would be found that certain poems required to be put in a class by themselves: poems in which, as with music, content is absorbed or dissolved in overwhelmingly powerful form. For the purpose of such classification (not to be attempted here, except for some poems in the extreme class just mentioned) it would be necessary to confine ourselves to that aspect of form which is common to music and poetry, as well as to the other arts, and to life and nature—that is, rhythm.

Consider a passage of indisputably authentic poetry:

The Approach by Form

Our revels now are ended. These our actors,
As I foretold you, were all spirits, and
Are melted into air, into thin air.
And, like the baseless fabric of this vision,
The cloud-capped towers, the gorgeous palaces,
The solemn temples, the great globe itself,
Yea, all which it inherit, shall dissolve
And, like this insubstantial pageant faded,
Leave not a rack behind. We are such stuff
As dreams are made on, and our little life
Is rounded with a sleep.

The irresistible effect of transport produced by these lines is due chiefly to the movement of the verse. No small part indeed comes from the magical words; but these are themselves an effect of form, for the rhythmical movement, taking its rise in aesthetic emotion, came first to the poet's mind, and the words were born to embody it. Now this is something more than normal verse form. In the majority of even excellent poetry the verse form delights but does not, in itself and by itself, powerfully move the reader. But in some poetry the aesthetic exaltation under which it was written has produced out of the common elements of metre and sense-stress a rhythmic form which conveys a similar exaltation to the reader, in a way familiar to those who listen to music. The temptation to call this kind of poetry "pure poetry" must be resisted, if for no other reason than that George Moore appropriated the term for a totally different species. (But it is interesting to notice that Mr. Louis Macneice uses the expression "impure poetry" to describe the "new" verse, which is the antithesis of the kind of poetry I have in mind just now.) "Pure lyric" is a better name for our kind, since it stresses, in the derivation of "lyric" from "lyre", the kinship with music which is the differentiating quality. "Pure lyric" is poetry that affects us like music (though producing also other effects unknown to music) by means of a rhythm which we may call "pure form". Since even the greatest poetry does not always exhibit this quality it cannot perhaps be regarded as a quality of high significance, yet it is of unique interest for its alchemic power of transmuting common metal into gold, the common mind into the mind of the visionary. It is an integral part of the art of de la Mare.

The power of rhythmic form is best demonstrated in a minor poem. Observing it in the opening of the Third Book of *Paradise Lost*, or in the triumphant turn of the *Adonais*, or in the lines prefixed to *The Excursion*, we may think that what moves us is the sublimity of the theme. But if in a poem written for children about a harmless and rather ridiculous beast we find ourselves not walking but flying, and flying through upper regions of truth and beauty, we may be assured that what seems obvious is indeed so, namely that the strange effect of illumination has been brought about by some magic in the "form".

Nicholas Nye is a well-known favourite, and a delicious example of that affinity which our poet feels no less with the "lower animals" than with the spirit world. It is a much better donkey poem than the equally celebrated one by Chesterton, which is a poem not about a donkey but about G.K.C. But the thing which, even more than its humanity and its humour,

16

lifts *Nicholas Nye* into the class of great poetry is its
verse-music.

It begins very quietly, and the first stanza goes to a
pleasant but unpretentious lilt till the note of "form"
comes suddenly in the unexpected short last line:

> And nobody there my lone to share
> But Nicholas Nye.

There is a sort of catch in the breath, and we find
ourselves taken on the flood of a low and magic
rhythm—

> Nicholas Nye was lean and grey,
> Lame of a leg and old—

that swings us along unresisting to the marvellous
climax at the end of the third stanza:

> But a wonderful gumption was under his skin,
> And a clear calm light in his eye,
> And once in a while, he'd smile,
> Would Nicholas Nye.

And so we fall softly, rhythmically down through

> Bony and ownerless, widowed and worn,
> Knobble-kneed, lonely and grey,

to the final whisper,

> Would brood like a ghost, and as still as a post,
> Old Nicholas Nye.

17

The Poetry of Reality

These excerpts are intended only to diversify an exposition. It is necessary to read the whole poem, and to surrender oneself to the rhythm, to perceive how the potency of form has elevated a charming animal study into a poem of enduring joy and significance.

It will have been noticed that at the rhythmic climax of this poem the rhythm was broken, and so intensified, by two sharp halts:

> And once in a while | he'd smile |
> Would Nicholas Nye.

Coleridge first discovered, and exhibited in the opening lines of *Christabel*, the surprising emotional effect of a hesitating movement in metre, and a century later de la Mare, so closely akin to Coleridge in poetic material, has taken this metrical element and used it to even subtler purpose. It may be seen in its most obvious but not least disturbing form in *The Song of the Mad Prince*. The terrible beauty and power of this poem are perhaps not fully capable of explanation, but the piercing, brain-shattering grief and loss that are its theme are brought to a pitch of almost intolerable intensity by the sudden stop, the unavoidable long pause, that occurs before the last line of each stanza. After the lines—

> Who said, "Where sleeps she now?
> Where rests she now her head
> Bathed in eve's loveliness?"—

there is a long hushed pause while the Mad Prince

looks wildly round until his head comes trembling
back to you and he leans towards you and whispers—

> That's what *I* said.

And again at the end of the second stanza: the voice
breaks in the penultimate line, where the words com-
pel a halting cadence,

> Life's | troubled | bubble | broken;

and then there is another age-long pause before the
despairing cry is again wrung from him—

> That's what I said.

(I let this interpretation of the poem, arrived at some
years ago, stand, but wish now to admit that it ignores
the strong suggestion of something diviner than grief
in the realization that the lost one "sleeps" and
"rests" in "loveliness" and in "all Time's delight",
now that life's troubles are left behind. It is the negative peace of Wordsworth's second stanza, "No
motion has she now", made positive and vital.)

But the supreme example of the use of the hesitation motif is to be seen in *The Listeners*. This poem,
the most popular and one of the greatest of de la
Mare's poems, has been the subject of many metrical
studies. Here we are less concerned with metre than
with the more comprehensive movement that uses
metre as one of its instruments. Miss Marguerite
Wilkinson suggests that the time of *The Listeners* is

set, and was set for the poet, by the first line—

> Is there anybody there? said the Traveller.

I think we must read on to the third and fourth lines before we catch the queer, uncanny music to which the poem is written. It is impossible to read these lines without sharp pauses at the places marked:

> And his horse | in the silence | champed | the grasses
> Of the forest's | ferny | floor.

At once we see that the whole poem goes to this staccato measure:

> Is there anybody | there? | said the Traveller,
> Knocking | on the moonlit | door.
> And his horse | in the silence | champed | the grasses
> Of the forest's | ferny | floor.
> And a bird | flew up | out | of the turret
> Above | the Traveller's | head. . . .

And at once the atmosphere grows strange, breathless, ghostly; skin creeps, hair begins to rise; the poet's mood is ours. The poet's aesthetic passion prompted this hesitating form, and form induces in us the passion of the poet.

The subtlety of the effect and its means may be marked by a comparison with *Arabia*, which is, metrically, a preliminary sketch for *The Listeners*. The metre is the same but the "form" is different. Instead of hesitation there is a smooth gliding movement, and the result is not eerieness but a magic of a less disturbing kind. It is easy for an imperceptive reader to deliver the lines of *The Listeners* in something of this smoother way, and consequently to miss the whole significance of the poem. Forrest Reid notes the queer movement, and calls it syncopation. As to the metre itself, without offering much to what others have done on the subject, I think the secret lies first in the maximum of variation that has been applied to the simple form, and second in the fact that the form is not so simple as it seems. (A metrical analysis of the poem will be found, by those who are interested in such things, at the end of the chapter.)

If it is possible to apply the term "objective" to any of de la Mare's poetry, *The Listeners* is perhaps the most wonderful example of his writing in that kind. Purely subjective is *The Tryst* (a)*, which again depends for its supreme power on form. The theme is one of the many perturbations in love's "extreme sad delight". This is presented in a series of fantastic and incredible images, so that, like the noblest music, the poem must be known by heart before its spell can operate. But having familiarized the strange conceptions, the reader can surrender himself to the movement of the verse. The hesitation motif (a lesser kind, and limited in its emotional range) is quite absent. What we have is a swaying, surging rhythm that sweeps us in a succession of great waves up to a climax not only of transcendent loveliness but of infinite poetic rapture:

* Here we have the first instance of de la Mare's duplicated titles. For method of reference see Preface, page xii.

Think, in Time's smallest clock's minutest beat
Might there not rest be found for wandering feet?
Or 'twixt the sleep and wake of a Helen's dream
Silence wherein to sing Love's requiem?

There is no means of representing the rhythmic movement of these four lines, nor the waves of rhythm—
lesser ones grouping themselves within larger ones,
incomparably varied yet disciplined and obedient to
the master rhythm of the whole—that precede. But their
nature and their power are such that one can abandon all
but a subconscious sense of the meaning of the separate
parts of the poem, and yet find oneself, at the climax, on
the heights of exaltation and mystical understanding.

The poet drops us from this climax of beauty into
four concluding lines of simple and satisfying paradox

.... Somewhere there Nothing is, and there lost man
Shall win what changeless vague of peace he can.

This is interesting but unimportant. The poem was
presented in the form of a question: an answer was
required: aesthetically any answer would have done.
The tremendous achievement of the poem is quite
apart from this. It is to have taken one of the richest
of human experiences as it shaped itself in the heart of
a great poet, and to have identified us with it by the
magic of rhythmic utterance.*

It cannot be too much insisted that what is here

* Compare de la Mare in the introductory essay to *Behold This
Dreamer:* "If music is the most perfect of the arts because it is least
diluted, and if poetry most closely approach music when it is most
poetic, when its sounds, that is, and the utterance of them and when
its rhythms rather than the words themselves, are its real if cryptic
language, any other meaning, however valuable it may be, is only a
secondary matter."

done is something unique, and something that could
only be done in this way. The emotional experience
which is the theme of *The Tryst* is akin to, or an element in, the far more complicated situation behind
Meredith's series of poems called *Modern Love*. That
situation is presented with great power, with genius.
But what Meredith has done in his poem-sequence
could have been done—though not so well, or not so
economically—in prose. Prose could not even begin
to do what is done in *The Tryst*. For a parallel—and, of
course, something more—one must go to a Beethoven
Sonata: say the D minor, Opus 31.2.

These are examples of the command of rhythmic
form which de la Mare possesses more completely
than any other modern poet. It is too potent a magic
to be employed at full power very frequently: its exercise must drain the magician's strength. Two things
have to be remembered about poetry of this kind
(though they apply almost equally to all true poetry):
pains must be taken to discover and follow the movement designed by the poet; and to convey this movement to the ear requires reading of a very high order.
It is not always realized that reading aloud is as difficult a business as playing the violin; complete success
in the one art, as in the other, necessitates gift, good
instrument, long training, and constant practice.*

* This fact is given practical recognition by the various verse-
speaking societies that now exist, but is not always kept in mind
when readers are being chosen for B.B.C. and other poetry readings.
Nevertheless the poetry readings held at the Lyric Theatre, Ham-
mersmith, and elsewhere during 1945 and 1946 (de la Mare himself taking a prominent part in some of them) constitute a cultural
development of the highest promise.

In the absence of reading of this order the music of these poems is best listened to with the inward ear.

A poem which perhaps owes some of its popularity to the ease with which its music can be rendered aloud is *The Sunken Garden*. There is here much of that other dellamarian quality, loveliness of word, and the power of the verse does not catch you (though it is hinted in the two opening lines) until you reach the second of the two stanzas. But at this point the enchanted rhythm blends subtly with the dream fancies, and the two become one music, as the ghost-children,

> Faintly swinging, sway and sweep,
> Like lovely sea-flowers in its deep.

The poem is de la Mare in little, with its children, its dreams, its loveliness, its perfection and power of form.

That marvellous poem, *The Song of Finis*, which fitly closes *Peacock Pie*, owes its indescribable effect to many factors. Like the famous couplet from the *Ode to a Nightingale*,

> Magic casements opening on the foam
> Of perilous seas in faery lands forlorn,

it brings a sudden satisfying breath from the world of romance. But whereas Keats gets his effect purely by bringing together a handful of beautiful words all crammed with romantic association, de la Mare, employing this factor more sparingly, gets his effect ultimately, I think, by the exquisitely varied move-

ment of the lines. After a prelusive first stanza (prelusive only in the musical sense now in question) the
second opens *cantabile*, and soon shows again the
skilful use of pause:

> No bird above that steep of time
> Sang of a livelong quest;
> No wind | breathed |
> Rest.

The slow calm of those few words accentuates the
swiftness and ardour of the next two lines—

> "Lone for an end!" cried knight to steed,
> Loosed an eager rein—

and the level force of the one that follows—

> Charged with his challenge into space;

so that the exaltation, as of a Sursum Corda, needs
only the benediction of the muted close—

> And quiet did quiet remain.

All the poems so far mentioned have been taken
from what may be called the early poems. During the
years between *Motley* (1918) and the publication of
The Burning-Glass in 1946 de la Mare virtually laid
aside that special lyric movement which I have called
"pure form", although it could not be altogether sup-
pressed. A cold and finished art characterizes the
poetry of the inter-war years, and it is in itself so ad-

mirable that it seemed stupid for the most fervent
lover of the earlier work to expect, or even to wish for,
the return of those "elfin rhythms", of what Humbert
Wolfe sensitively described as "that dropped syllable,
like a dropped heart-beat, that set the blood running
thin and fresh". And then, in 1945, when de la Mare
was seventy-two, a quite extraordinary thing hap-
pened: *The Burning-Glass*, which appeared in that
year, is infused with the spirit, and to some extent
with the intense lyric force, of *The Listeners* and *Motley*. There are many readers who prefer the de la Mare
of the *Veil-Memory* years to the singing poet whose
meaning lay in his music (just as there are those who
prefer the later Yeats and the Conrad of *Nostromo*).
But that there have been an earlier and a later de la
Mare there is no denying. And it is to be remembered
that very few poets have continued to write after forty
the poetry they wrote before reaching that age. Certainly I do not know any poet who has made a come-
back comparable to this one. Not, of course, that all
the poems of *The Burning-Glass* are in the older manner. More than half belong properly to the later
period, including the two which have been most ad-
mired, *The Scarecrow* and *The Ditch*. But there are a
number of poems—enough, for one with a listening
ear, to set the tone of the volume—in which passionate
vision is carried on a passionate music, and the vision
and the poem and the music are one. I have said
enough on this theme, but I may instance *Two Gardens*, where introspective intensity moves on a full
gliding current of lovely words; *To a Candle*, another
crystal stream of wonder and ecstasy; *The Owl* (c),

whose delicate rhythms recall the pure magic of *The Scribe*; *Ariel* (b), *The Vision*, *The Rainbow* (b). . . . The poet himself points us to the aesthetic principle involved, in the last stanza of *The Summons*:

> . . . notes like these, sad, urgent, sweet,
> Call from an Egypt named the heart,
> Which with a deeper life doth beat
> Than any wherein thought hath part.

De la Mare's mastery of rhythmic movement has always been recognized, but the quality itself has been a little undervalued. Literary criticism is always too ready to adopt the standards of Aristotle and Matthew Arnold, neglecting the more truly aesthetic approach of Longinus and Charles Lamb. It is perhaps not the only but it is certainly the first requirement of poetry that it should delight, and the delightfulness of de la Mare, which would nowhere be denied, is the rare delight of a new sensation—one that has been sufficiently characterized in the foregoing pages: the sensation engendered by great music, and by some architecture, sculpture and pictures. The delight is not one of the ear alone: it is "felt in the blood and felt along the heart", and echoes in every chamber of the mind, moving it to secret and creative harmony. And the harmony is that of the poet's mind, for the rhythm that moved the poet moves us in the same way. It is only partly true to say that the rhythm of a poem follows or arises from the method of the poet's thought or feeling. It is probably a more accurate representation of the way things hap-

27

pen to say that the poet's thought arises from the rhythmic motions of his mind. Accordingly, if he can set up similar rhythmic motions in the mind of the reader, a state of consciousness will be induced in the reader in which the poet's thought, as expressed in the words of the poem, will mean to the reader exactly (perhaps it would be safer to say approximately) what it meant to the poet. Mr. I. A. Richards says, "An extraordinarily intricate concourse of impulses brings the words (of a poem) together. Then in another mind the affair in part reverses itself: the words bring into being a similar concourse of impulses. . . . Why this should happen is still something of a mystery". Mystery it is likely to remain, like other "whys" of art, but the mechanism of the process (as it operates in the case of "pure lyric") is explained by the "rhythmic" suggestions I have just offered, and is analogous to that of the making and playing of a gramophone record. The "intricate concourse of impulses" rhythmic in themselves cuts its groove of rhythmic form on the matrix of language, and afterwards, if the aesthetic sense of the reader follows the rhythmic form as closely as the needle follows the groove on the gramophone record, the original "concourse of impulses" gets reproduced in his mind with more or less exactness according to the capacity and receptivity of that mind.

All successful metre facilitates this identification, this complete understanding between poet and reader, in its own degree. That de la Mare sometimes employs a metrical form so enriched and modified as to have become almost a new medium, is doubtless due to the rarity of the imaginative material with which he

wishes to interpenetrate our minds, the remoteness
of his poetic life and experience from anything we
have known. What he has to do is something more
than to bring about that "willing suspension of un-
belief" which is the aim of all writers whose themes
are of the supernatural order. After all, every man
carries about with him his own little supernatural
world—of dreams, faiths and fancies, and is tolerant
of the greater but kindred wonders offered to his gaze.
But not only is de la Mare more completely "access-
ible to dream" than any other poet; there is in addition
the peculiar difficulty of his dream world, that it
throws a transparency of dream over the world of
waking life, making the "real" and the "unreal" one.
You never know which world you are in, because de
la Mare does not distinguish two worlds at all. Death
wagging his key at the child looking out of the
window is as actual as the shadow that produced the
"illusion", but no more actual, and therefore to the
child merely an object of equal curiosity. Two other
modern writers who thus habitually confuse the two
worlds are Mr. James Stephens and Lord Dunsany.
Both employ the weapon of humorous prose to induce
us to accept their ambiguous landscape. De la Mare's
purpose is deeper than even humour will take him, so
he brings into operation the strange powers that lie in
rhythmic form.

> When music sounds, gone is the world I know,
> And all her lovely things even lovelier grow. . . .

The effect of rhythmic form in poetry is something
like this—due allowance being made not only for the

greater power of music but for the difference between de la Mare and the general reader! Under its influence the beauty and truth, the wonder and delight, presented to us in the poem grow more intense, more urgent, and the illusion (if it be but that) is created that the limitations of the senses are suddenly freed, that the barriers set up by the imperfections of thought between the soul and ultimate reality are down. Indeed, as we saw in Chapter I, it is necessary to believe that it is no matter of illusion. There *is* reality: it is something other than appearance: the poet, by his art, makes us aware of it, and perhaps enables us to understand a little of its nature. A poem like *A Sunday* may be made out of items—a child, a river, a "Sabbath peace"—so elemental as to seem to us eternal, but it is the form of the poem, woven of music and silence, speaking half to the ear and half to the heart—with its unsubtle yet cunningly varied metre, now swaying, now falling away, now hesitating, now repeating—that brings upon us the very breath of eternity itself.

This is the mystical power of form. But it has a physical aspect of almost equal interest. The unimpassioned varieties of literature produce mental reactions only. As rhythm enters, the appeal extends to the physical side. At first, in poetry and rhythmic prose, this takes the form of a delighting of the ear. But in pure lyric the rhythmic movement is strangely close and direct in its action: there is a pressing, a lifting force which seems quite definite of bodily operation. While retaining all its hold upon the aesthetic emotions, which must be spiritual in their nature, pure lyric simultaneously and equally moves the physical side. What makes this form of poetry seize us with such mastery is the violence with which it forces that gate, the physical, by which penetration to our central fastnesses is still most readily effected. Indeed, the criterion of the effect of pure form is pain. Not the divine despair produced by all great art—the sense of the immeasurable gulf that separates us from such achievement or conception. That sense is a mental impression: the pain I speak of is objectively sensible, and helps to assign to pure lyric its place with other supreme manifestations of beauty, whether of art or of nature. For just this sensation comes swiftly and strangely to the heart as some vision of lake or woodland breaks upon the sight.

> Green in light are the hills. . . .
> Coloured with buds of delight the boughs are swaying,
> Beauty walks in the woods. . . .

And who has not, walking round an inoffensive corner in Oxford, been left weak by the vivid stabbing beauty of a grey-black miracle in stone? Beauty has many modes, of which one is rhythmic form; the first and most direct appeal of all of them is physical, and its characteristic is pain.

This was sometime a paradox; but it is one of Nature's paradoxes, and not to be denied. For delving into causes this is not the place. Perhaps a flicker of race-consciousness—"Beauty, that must die". Perhaps a sense of fear arising from pity: perfection looks so frail and defenceless amid the seething mass of the brutally efficient second-rate. Perhaps, on the other

31

hand, a sense of fear as at the suddenly realized presence of a god:

> "for 'tis the eternal law
> That first in beauty should be first in might."

Or perhaps simply the tendency of exquisite pleasure and exquisite pain to shade indistinguishably into each other. Whatever the cause, the sharp pang of beauty is the first warning of her presence, and in literature rhythmic form is the pure essence of beauty.

*   *   *

But it is time to take some notice of de la Mare's handling of form in the more superficial sense, of his craftsmanship. Here, within the limits of lyric type, he exhibits, generally, a perfection of art as flawless as Tennyson's. It is interesting to observe how this was achieved. The first volume, *Songs of Childhood*, published in 1902, shows none of this perfection of craftsmanship, but is rich in those delights that presently came to be recognized as characteristic de la Mare, though the final magic of rhythm is there only as an undertone. *Poems* 1906 marks a great advance in art, and yet is deeply disappointing when read immediately after the 1902 volume, because it contains so little of that entirely new thing—the spirit of Walter de la Mare—that made *Songs of Childhood* so precious. It seems that the poet was consciously disciplining himself to an exquisite artistry, but achieving this at a cost, giving us a greater number of excel-

32

lent poems than were in the earlier volume, but very few to be remembered with equal pleasure. Yet the cost was well worth while. For in the first place, out of this conscious artistry was perfected the ultimate music of rhythmic form, embodied here in just one or two examples—*Age*, and *The Phantom* (b). Moreover, the discipline of this volume was so effective that perfection of art became a habit, and in the next three volumes, far from being an obstacle to those special things this poet was born to create, it became the necessary medium and final voice of their utterance. Where, in a sublunary and slipshod world, are there to be found jewels more miraculously cut than *Shadow*, *Remembrance*, and *England*, from *Poems* 1906, unless it be *The Three Cherry Trees*, *Noon and Night Flower*, and *The Dwelling Place*, from *The Listeners?* *The Dwelling Place* is a longer poem than usual, but is no less exquisitely finished. With the poem before you, observe first the shapely handling of the theme: how after the first "Alas" comes a "Yet" introducing an antithesis that occupies the rest of the poem up to the last stanza, when another antithesis deftly turns us back to our starting-point. Observe how symmetrically the body of the theme, between the two "yets", is plotted: three stanzas to pure joy, three (one omitted in *Collected Poems*) to the shadowy hints of sorrow, three to the terror that came by night. Observe particularly in this third triad, the climax of the poem, how beautifully the parallelism proceeds: the door barred, the three-fold curtain, the candles and the songs; the one face gone, the doubt and the dark, the shadow at the door and the faint reiterated call: with minor internal balancings—heavy door and lightfoot fear, bright fire and dark wine, the dark night and the painted wall. Every stanza in the poem —each one perfectly maintaining the line yet each with its own strongly marked variations of pause or scansion—might be separately examined for exquisitely painted miniatures, jewelled lines, chosen epithets. And all this "art" without detriment to the magically conceived theme, rising and falling with rhythmic life.

It has been suggested above that de la Mare's mastery of the formal side of his art was deliberately attained in the 1906 volume. Among the evidences of conscious effort are the exercises in two forms not natural to him, blank verse and the sonnet; and it is here that we have his only failures in form. This is interesting, because the rule is that good poets either write good blank verse or are wise enough to avoid it altogether. The ability to write a good sonnet is by no means universal, but I should say that every poet since Shakespeare has written blank verse, if at all, of an excellence roughly commensurate with his poetic genius. In the nature of things de la Mare should have been, and in the main is, one of those who leave the unrhymed species alone. He needs rhyme as Walter Scott needed his button. The blank verse adopted for the Shakespeare characters is quite lifeless. As one makes an exception in favour of the delicious *Mercutio* one notices that there is here a hint of a rhyme or so, which seems to have made all the difference; and certainly the series was well worth while if it led to the perfect line—

34

Leaving the Spring faint with Mercutio.

A more flexible blank verse is used for the later poem *Heresy*.

Unlike Wordsworth, de la Mare draws no strength from the discipline of the sonnet form. The few early sonnets are undistinguished; of later ones, *In the Dock* expresses with great power that social pity which is a prime motive of the volume in which it appeared, but has not the special characteristics of a sonnet; *A Young Girl* has a perfect first quatrain but is again perhaps not quite unified in its thought; the sonnet called *Peace* comes nearest to perfection—the octave fault-less, with its lovely opening,

> Night is o'er England and the winds are still,

its view widening to "the stars that are all Europe's", and narrowing again to the dead beneath the churchyard trees.

De la Mare's ability to express in marvellous verse all the marvellous things he has to say is excelled by few even of the greatest poets. Moreover, it is pro-gressive, and in *Motley* it is absolute. In this volume, as in *Hamlet*, content and form are perfectly balanced, and not to be distinguished. Here we find profound imaginative vision given utterance in poem after poem of flawless art: *The Linnet, The Sunken Garden, The Tryst* (a), *The Ghost* (b), *Music* (a), *The Remon-strance, Vigil, The Scribe, Fare Well*, many others.

Most of these poems are examined elsewhere, but let us look for a moment at *Music*. Here again is the magic of form: the subtlest and most secret of de la Mare's reactions to music are conveyed to the reader through the power and passion of the metre, with its swift crescendoes and slower cadences, its movement now held up by spondees, now released in dactyls, its three stanzas, built round the three words *flame, dream, haunt,* growing in intensity to the last of those words and then sinking suddenly away. But how well does even the surface meaning of the poem transcribe the power of music to fade out all of life that is not music, to turn loveliness into a vision and beauty into a dream, to make us aware, as nothing else, not even poetry, can, of that shadowy other world, our lost inheritance.

Here, in this poem, as in the other poems comprehended under the thesis of this chapter, we may see exemplified that definition of poetry given by de la Mare in *Behold This Dreamer* (pp. 104-5): it is worth setting beside the older and more famous definitions: to secure it de la Mare has looked long and minutely, with expert eye, into himself, into the soul of a poet.

> "All lyrical poetry beats with the heart, tells of things seen and felt in a sudden clearness of the senses, and with a flame in the thought. An insatiable delight in life haunts it, and the keen mortal regret that stalks in life's shadow. It springs from a height of living . . . a tension of spirit, a sense of wonder and mystery, a faith in all that is held most dear, a hope and hunger for an unknown that transcends the known."

*　　*　　*

The Approach by Form

To elaborate what was said on page 21 about the metrical form of *The Listeners* being "not so simple as it seems".* The apparent three-foot lines are really five-foot lines in disguise. It is easy enough to scan

> Is there ánybody thére said the tráveller
> Knócking on the móonlit dóor

as anapaestic trimeter with an extra syllable or two, but no one ever heard of feet such as this formula necessitates for the line

> Fell é | choing through the shá | dowiness of the stíll house.

Undoubtedly the lines are all to be read with three stresses but the actual framework of the metre has five:

> Is there án | ybód | y thére | —sáid | the tráveller.

This makes the polysyllabic line more manageable:

> Fell é | choing thróugh | the shád | owiness óf | the stíll house.

* Some readers will feel metrical analysis of a poem like *The Listeners* to be both distasteful and destructive. For me it increases the interest and delight of the poem. Sir Walford Davies used to take (alas! that he can no longer take) the daintiest rondo to pieces, phrase by phrase, and not destroy it; it does no harm to know that Chartres and Ely did not, in fact, grow from the ground, but are the result of a process of one stone being placed on another with great precision and in strict accordance with the laws of building construction. As for the type of scansion, I use the old Saintsburian method because it is the one I am most accustomed to, but also because it still seems to me to fit traditional verse, such as de la Mare's, better than any of the modern schemes, which are often merely alternatives to Saintsbury.

37

The Poetry of Reality

The shorter lines are subject to the same complication, for, however the poem is scanned, odd and even lines are metrically equal. For the five-foot measure the even lines have to be eked out with pauses, and the staccato effect noticed is the result of the action and reaction of these pauses. Thus metrically we have—

of the fór | ... èst's | ...férn | ... ỳ | ...flóor,

but in reading these pauses get bunched: the first joins the second, the third joins the fourth, producing these powerful and significant stops which gave us the clue to the poem's rhythmic form:

Of the fórest's ... férny ... flóor.

This is what gives verse-music, particularly in English, its infinite subtlety and variability—that three stresses, metrical stress, rhythmic stress, and sense-stress, are mingled.

CHAPTER III

The Beauty of Words

WORDS are the link between form and content. They have a foot in either camp. The poet's mastery of form is like the musician's technique, words are the instrument he plays on; and as much care goes to the making, selection and treatment of the poet's vocabulary as of a Steinway or a Cremona. It is a distinguishing quality of a good singer to be always "plumb in the middle of the note", and this vocal position corresponds to the poet's verbal nicety. The "inevitable" word, indeed, is rather a feature of prose, where the word that amazes us does so by its marvellous rightness of meaning or appropriateness. The poet's word startles not infrequently by its remoteness, not so much pronouncing final truth as opening up new possibilities of content, adding new shades of significance. "Golden lads and girls" . . . "She was a phantom of delight" . . . "I will live thy Protestant to be" . . . "the bottom of the monstrous world" . . . "the dawn comes up like thunder". This, I think, is what Longinus meant when he said beautiful words were the light of the mind. The word comes before the thought, and by its illumination we see the unexpected. In poetry the beauty of a word is more important than its truth, for if the word is sufficiently beautiful it creates a new truth of its own. Violets were not dim nor stars earnest till Keats and Shakespeare called them so. Whereever we open de la Mare, there are few poets of whom

39

his own dictum (*Behold This Dreamer*) is more true: "A poem . . . is exquisitely at liberty in a cage of words which it is . . . a joy to examine."

There are no beautiful words. Words become beautiful by use. The form of the name Helen is quite plain, yet by age-long association it has gathered to itself a dazzling brightness, an epical stature. The word "rose", especially in the hands of a Yeats or a Tennyson, seems as beautiful as the flower it names, but in sound it is no better than "nose". De la Mare somewhere points out that the word "mother" is not intrinsically beautiful. So many things go to condition beauty in words. Sound is less important than association, and appearance has a good deal to do with it. Hence the aesthetic objection to reformed spelling, and the greater charm of Spenser in the old guise:

> Sweet Themmes, run foftly till I end my fong.

But it is the way in which words are combined (as with notes in music) that finally decides their beauty. "Wages" is an ugly word in sound, in appearance, and (unfortunately) by association; but it becomes a thing of perfect beauty in the song from *Cymbeline*, or in Henley's lines—

> So be my passing!
> My task accomplished and the long day done,
> My wages taken, and in my heart
> Some late lark singing. . . .

See, as I suggested above, what cunning repetition does for "rose"—

40

The Beauty of Words

Ah! a rose!
A rose, one rose, by those fair fingers culled. . . .

or—

Red Rose, proud Rose, sad Rose of all my days.

De la Mare is a millionaire of beautiful words,
single or in combination. He lives in a world of beauty,
and a harsh word, one feels, would be wrenched from
him like an aching tooth. To the rule recently cited,
that there are no intrinsically beautiful words, obvious
exceptions start to the mind. One of them is "lovely".
It cannot be spoilt by being put into the mouth of a
gaping maid-servant and spelt "luvly". It flutters in
the hand like a little captured bird. It is (or was for
long), with its substantive, "loveliness", de la Mare's
favourite word. One is reminded of the fact that Mr.
Masefield's favourite word is "beauty"; half the
difference between the two poets is symbolized in the
two facts. Someone has said, "Loveliness is beauty
robbed of its terribleness. Beauty is sharp and stabbing, loveliness is tranquil. . . . Beauty is like sex in
that it excites. Loveliness is a benediction, and brings
a peace that passes understanding".

It is interesting to note the result that comes out
when one tries to justify the impression mentioned,
that "lovely" is de la Mare's favourite epithet. If we
count the occurrences of "lovely" and "loveliness" in
Motley we shall find they number eleven. But we shall
have noticed by the way that "beauty" and "beautiful", which we supposed to be less characteristic, are
used twenty-one times. Is the impression therefore

41

mistaken? No. "Beauty" is of the staple of poetic
diction. All normal poetry makes frequent use of it.
What distinguishes de la Mare is the high ratio of
"lovely" to "beautiful" in his work: it is, as shown
above, 1 :2. If the sonnets of Shakespeare contained in
Palgrave's Golden Treasury are examined in the
same way there will be found two examples of
"lovely" and ten of "beautiful", giving a ratio of 1 :5,
while Shakespeare's own favourite word, "sweet",
occurs seven times. As for Masefield, the *Lollingdon
Downs* sonnets contain three examples of "lovely" to
fifty-seven of "beautiful", a ratio of 1 :19.

Another word,* more consciously "poetic", and
continuously characteristic of de la Mare, is "tranquil".

> The sky was like a water-drop
> In shadow of a thorn,
> Clear, tranquil, beautiful,
> Forlorn.

No one else can use words quite like that. Is it not
miraculous? What affluence, yet what economy, of art
that can pack into four brief lines a supreme simile,
two unforgettable pictures, and no less than four
perfect epithets.† The stanza is like some wonderful

*Others are "transient" and "lonely" with their variants.

† This is how the stanza stood as originally printed in 1906. In
the Collected Edition of 1942 the fourth line reads, "Dark, forlorn".
This means either that "beautiful" has been re-scanned as "beautiful", with "dark", completing the tetrameter: "Clear, tranquil
beautiful, dark"; or that a half-hearted attempt has been made to
bring the first stanza into line with the other three: but to do this
fully would require a *sixth* epithet!—e.g.

piece of glass that a connoisseur picks up and lightly flicks with his finger-nail: the high, pure note floats out on the air: de la Mare, the connoisseur, listens enchanted. The remaining three stanzas of the poem (*Remembrance*, from *Poems* 1906, the volume where de la Mare's art is more deliberate than elsewhere among the earlier work) complete the delicate word-pattern. This is not de la Mare's highest art. It is the art of a still life by Chardin, which, though nothing but a representation of a vase, a bowl, a spoon and a few globules of fruit, opens a little window on the infinite.

Many of these comparatively early poems, especially perhaps those into which rhythmic form does not enter strongly, are clustered with starry words. That microscopic marvel, *Old Shellover* (which, if it alone survived of de la Mare's work, would make posterity know that here had been a great poet), owes its final magic to a catch of rhythm, but owes not a little to the *horny* old gardener and the *rising* moon.

> "Come!" said Old Shellover.
> "What?" says Creep.
> "The horny old gardener's fast asleep;
> The fat cock thrush
> To his nest has gone,
> And the dew shines bright
> In the rising moon;
> Old Sallie Worm from her hole doth peep.
> "Come!" said Old Shellover.
> "Ay!" said Creep.

> Clear, tranquil, beautiful,
> Tremulous, dark, forlorn.

Surely best to leave the original matchless four alone.

43

The Poetry of Reality

You must go to the songs of Shakespeare—from the *Dream* or the *Tempest*, say—for a parallel perfection. The art of *Then* is simpler, but not a word is out of place; or *Silver*—where de la Mare makes play with the genius of the English language. When the metals gold and silver were created, the words "golden" and "silver" were made to describe them, and so the poet simply lets a cascade of "silvers" and "silverys" shower down through the poem from the moon in the first line, and as they fall their white light is caught on bright words placed here and there about the poem— casements and fruit and the doves' white breasts, fish and water and the eye of a harvest mouse, so that the whole poem is a dazzle of light with its centre at the point where

> Couched in his kennel, like a log,
> With paws of silver sleeps the dog.

Similarly the *Song of Shadows*: an effect, an atmosphere, is aimed at, the embodiment of a moment when this world trembles on the brink of another; the effect is completely obtained, and obtained by a series of images: but the images are painted in words—and it would not have seemed possible to collect into so small a space so many words steeped in the atmosphere it is desired to evoke. There is no single word which, by sound or significance, breaks the spell.

> Sweep thy faint strings, Musician,
> With thy long lean hand;
> Downward the starry tapers burn. . . .

44

The Beauty of Words

Or how startlingly does one come, after half-a-dozen jolly children's rhymes, in the section of *Peacock Pie* called "Witches and Fairies", on that perfect poem of gramarye, *The Changeling*: its haunting force depends on the word, "Ahoy", which rings out clear and sweet in the first line,

> "Ahoy and ahoy!"
> 'Twixt mocking and merry,

and echoes down through the poem to die out in the last lines,

> You shall hear o'er the water
> Ring faint in the grey—
> "Ahoy and ahoy there!"
> And tremble away;
> "Ahoy and ahoy" . . . .
> And tremble away.*

The Listeners volume combines beauty of music and of word very completely. Martha, in the poem of that name, is one of de la Mare's exquisitely not-quite-human characters, but she is more than usually real though she holds the keys to fairyland. And both the delicious personality and the freedom of fairyland are created by a most happy choice of words and phrases: the "clear grey eyes", their "beautifulness tranquil as dreams", the "two slim hands", her "grave small

---

* A similar "other-world" effect is got from "Ahooh" in the last stanza of the poem *The Owl* (c) in *The Burning-glass*. That the effect is produced by word *plus music* is shown by the fact that the same cry at the end of the other *Owl* (b) poem, in *The Fleeting*, fails to bring the *crépuscule* around you in the same eerie way.

45

lovely head"; then the "fairies and gnomes" that "stole out in the leaf-green light", and her beauty "fading far away" as "her voice ran on". . . . "Once . . . once upon a time . . ." until

> Like clouds in the height of the sky
> Our hearts stood still in the hush
> Of an age gone by.

Winter, again, is a little sharp-etched picture, and the intense chiaroscuro is obtained by means of beautifully chosen words. And loveliest of all in this kind, that apotheosis of the mood of approaching night and sleep, *Nod*. One wonders how it was done. Every word, every syllable, every letter is so beautiful and so right that one can imagine the poem taking years to perfect, like the *Elegy*. And yet it flows and grows with such sweet ease and naturalness that it seems more likely to have been written, just as it is, at a sitting.

Other poems give profound beauty perfect expression in words of an exquisite simplicity. *The Scribe* is woven of words like "hand", "seed", "speech", "ant", "ink", "pen", and "Z"; and *Fare Well* is almost as plain: yet both poems touch the heights and depths of beauty and imaginative vision. Effects as great are achieved by means as simple in *The Linnet*, *The Ghost* (b), *Vigil*, and *For All the Grief* (though the diction of *The Sunken Garden*, *The Tryst* (a), and *Music* (a) is of sunset splendour). But indeed a certain quietness of utterance is characteristic of all de la Mare's poetry, and is of the very

46

essence of his word-quality. He has at no time made
it a practice to startle with a sudden brilliant word,
in the manner of Humbert Wolfe—

> Would ragged robin fail to make
> Her universal red mistake?—

or "the crawling inattention of the dust". De la
Mare's words seldom stand out individually; their
beauty is intense but unobtrusive.* Such a poem as
The Ogre reads like a ballad, but examination shows
something far different from the good ballad virtue of
plain narrative lit up by occasional flashes of inspiration. *The Ogre* is word perfect: the words, without
exception, are as exquisitely right, and as exquisitely
natural, as the notes of a Schubert song. And it is
only this quality raised to a higher power that gives
us those poems of a richer beauty that were used to
illustrate the earlier part of this chapter.

Sometimes, as in *The Hawthorn hath a Deathly
Smell*, he seems just to throw together a handful of
marvellous words, with thrilling effect;

> Eyes of all loveliness—
> Shadow of strange delight.

Or think of that picture from *The Ghost* (b):

> Silence. Still faint on the porch
> Brake the flames of the stars.

* Keats—"Poetry sh'd be great and unobtrusive. . . . Poetry
should surpass by a fine success, and not by singularity." (*Letters.*)

47

Observing the unusual word "flames", one observes
also how the whole tone of the picture depends on the
threefold repetition of the vowel-sound of that word.
Studies of vowel-sounds in poetry, even when done by
Miss Edith Sitwell, are more delightful than useful,
since it can generally be shown that the same arrangement of vowels in a different set of words produces a
different effect; otherwise something might be made
of the extraordinary diversity of vowel-sounds in the
poem, *The Listeners:* hardly a line contains the same
sound twice. And though Mr. Robert Graves (I
think) felt the assonance in

> Through what wild centuries
> Roves back the rose

to be unfortunate, it is possible to feel on the other
hand that the half-completed echo matches the
romantic thought, just as the "wild" of centuries is
a sort of proleptic echo of an unheard "wild" before
"rose".

I have said that, in a general way, association and
meaning have more to do with the beauty of words
than sound. In particular instances de la Mare suggests that the contrary is true. Just as the movement
of a line may carry more of its author's intention than
is to be found in its verbal sense, so de la Mare is insistent that the sound of a word may have its own
supreme significance. Naming certain beautiful and
antique words he asks us to

> Whisper their syllablings till all meaning is gone,
> And sound all vestige loses of mere word. . . .

and to watch for the effect. This is perhaps what

Humbert Wolfe meant when he said that with de la Mare words in themselves have an almost absolute value. Wolfe was referring to the later poems (after 1918), and certain it is that in the later books words are used in a new way. They no longer grow like blue-bells in a wood, but are chosen (perhaps for their "absolute value") and placed like the pieces of a mosaic. Thus, of a later "Shellover"—

> Then, all your wreathéd house astir,
> Horns reared, grim mouth, deliberate pace,
> You glide in silken silence where
> The feast awaits your grace.

But the choice is not always so successful. Compare *The Old Angler* with what was said above about *The Ogre*. *The Old Angler* is a superb poem, and leaves an unforgettable dream-picture on the mind: its creative factor is intensity of feeling; nothing or little, I think, is given by the diction, while expressions like "Huddled in pensive solitariness" or "His tanned cheek greyed" stand up like snags in the stream. (The influence of Hardy is seen here and in a few other poems.)

That in all ways perfect poem, *A Dull Boy*, where the poet, modestly disclaiming any idea that the making of poetry can be called work, hopes that when the Judge asks him, "And what didst *thou?*" . . . and the heavens listen for his reply, "the lost child" in him will cry bravely, "Play!"—contains in its first stanza a second and more succinct definition of poetry, as a

> stubborn desperate quest
> To conjure life, love, wonder into words.

"Stubborn desperate quest" is a formula applicable to the spiritual necessity of the poet's life: as a description of the technical side of poetry it seems to differentiate the art of the later poems; the art of the earlier poems is beautifully suggested by the two lines which complete the stanza:

> Far happier songs than any me have blest
> Were sung, at ease, this daybreak by the birds.

The connection between rhythmic form and beautiful words is variable. Of two quatrains by Wordsworth, one has rhythmic form, the other has not;

> Love had he found in huts where poor men lie;
> His daily teachers had been woods and rills,
> The silence that is in the starry sky,
> The sleep that is among the lonely hills.

Here, after the preparatory first two lines, we have two others which, with the profound pause after "silence", the swift movement, slowing down, of the next six words, and the calm, even, deliberate movement of the last line, seem to me to create an effect far beyond anything explicable by reference to the words and the sense. Now this:

> There sometimes doth a leaping fish
> Send through the tarn a lonely cheer;
> The crags repeat the raven's croak
> In symphony austere.

The effect of these lines comes entirely from the in-

dividual words and their associations, and it is hardly
less strong and vivid than that produced by the
Brougham Castle stanza, where the appeal is to a more
elemental aesthetic sense. Two stanzas from a de la
Mare poem, *Night* (a), will show again how slight
may be the connection between form and words.

> All from the light of the sweet moon
>   Tired men now lie abed,
> Actionless, full of vision, soon
>   Vanishing, soon fled.

> The starry night aflock with beams
>   Of crystal light scarce stirs:
> Only its birds, its cocks, the streams
>   Call, 'neath heaven's wanderers.

The words of the first stanza are quite commonplace,
yet rhythm wells up in the third and fourth lines,
owing to the arrangement of the pauses and the strong
accents on the first syllables of "actionless", "vision",
and "vanishing". The second stanza is more "poetic"
in its choice of words, but this is chiefly true of the
first two lines, whereas it is again in lines three and
four that rhythm becomes compelling, owing to the
distribution of stress and the retarding spondees. On
the other hand the potent magic of *The Pedlar* is undoubtedly due to the fact that the lilting, drowsy
rhythm is carried out in words of which almost every
one is lovely with special significance.

The form of a rose is in its bloom, but the bloom
lives by virtue of the hidden root. Behind the music

E   51

of the sonata there is the mind of Beethoven, with its strange thoughts, its infinite dreams, its passionate feeling. In a poem, the words are the evidence of the foundation of mind, the well-spring of the poet's aesthetic response to his theme. With many poets, often with de la Mare himself, the words—marvellous things, marvellously set out—must of themselves convey all that can be conveyed of the poet's mind, and the great poet can make them do it successfully. But words are so easily misunderstood. Words mean different things to different users of them. An association too many or too few, and the whole connotation of the word is changed. So the power of rhythm, with its more direct contact and its universal language, is invoked.

CHAPTER IV

The Visionary World

De la Mare is a "lyric poet". But that is an incomplete definition. The poets included in the *Golden Treasury* have a common factor, song, but are in other respects deeply differentiated. Lyric is by definition feeling plus music, and lyric of this kind we have to perfection in Herrick, Burns, Davies, and in lesser degree in scores of others. But lyric form will take in, and give out, more than this. It is not unusual, though it is not common, for the musical expression of intense feeling to lead to the mystic revelation which was the subject of earlier chapters. This happens continuously with Shakespeare, often with Wordsworth, sometimes with Shelley, Coleridge, Marvell, Blake, Tennyson, with Keats, in the *Odes* and *Hyperion*, with Arnold in some of his irregular monologues. Among later poets we have it frequently in Yeats and occasionally in Wolfe and Flecker. And it is by reason of his wide and—over some areas of his poetry—continuous display of this special lyric gift that de la Mare holds place with the masters of the more comprehensive forms. What Mr. A. C. Ward so well said about that exiguous poem, *The Scribe*— that it has all the depth and splendour of an epic—is equally true of a great number of his short poems, those in which the creative power of lyric form is most intense.

This brings me to the title of the present chapter,

which has been arrived at after some hesitation. I have spoken of that more real world to which the poet brings us by the power of lyric form or the magic of words. If then to such world we have been brought, we ought perhaps to be able to describe it, and this chapter should have been called "the world of Reality". But no! If Reality can be described at all it can only be in poetry (or music). And I am far from claiming that the poet actually shows us Reality itself. What he does is to show us the world of his mind: a world extraordinarily different from our world of "getting and spending", and one from whose mountain-tops we can, if the day is clear and our sight keen, see—or think we see—the spires and towers, the dazzling peaks and lighted skies, of that strange land that I have called Reality, as the Scholar Gypsy saw from Cumnor brow, dimly through the falling snow, the line of festal light in Christ Church Hall. Where dwells the poet's mind when it is busy with poetry, with what new knowledge is it equipped, what is the quality of its vision?

Poet's country is a place where Reality is felt to be very close—just on the other side of a door, as it were. Man, a lonely traveller, knocks upon the door but gets no answer. Nevertheless he is sufficiently sure that there is something behind that door to knock and ask his question before he goes on, leaving behind, on the one side, silence, on the other, something of which he knows only that it is spiritual in its nature. Or if, after long voyaging, he achieves the Grail of Knowledge, he dies in the next moment. Sometimes, through the vapid surface of day-to-day life, like the moon momentarily seen through enveloping cloud, he catches an actual glimpse of Reality, and perceives it to be an ecstasy. Can it be that life immortal is mortal life lived with supreme intensity? There are certain ladders which seem to climb towards the inaccessible world: one of them is dream. Dream is a state of consciousness in which the senses are cut off, leaving the mind free to use its nonsensuous faculties of perception. It operates with greater difficulty, though to better effect, in a state of waking (when we call it intuition), more commonly in sleep. Out of that mysterious condition called sleep, there "burgeons" a whole realm of enchantment, which lies beside the waking world, and may be the fringes of Reality confusedly experienced. The poet's dreams (which are not as our dreams) offer him an unearthly wisdom, but even the poet cannot hold that wisdom in his heart, though he burns with the desire to recapture it. Yet he has a tranquil smiling faith in the efficacy of dream: though it may find voice only in a few sweet songs, these come nearer to Reality than all the philosophies. Dream, fantasy, imagination are for the poet the very "breath of life".

Of extrinsic aids, music is the surest. The poet knows there is another life than that of the senses because music carries him bodily into it: his blinded eyes feast themselves on its loveliness—its flaming flowers, trees ecstatically still, Naiads with enchanted face. How can this life be all when music has such power upon the spirit, arresting the passage of time, shutting out sensation, giving meaning to the shadows, calling ghosts to linger in the darkening air? And next to music, the absence of music, of all sound—silence and stillness. When things usually full of movement and life—a house, a human being—are found all still and asleep, the effect may be one of an illuminating fear creeping cloudlike over the mind. The small continuous silence of swallows departed haunts the day like a vanished love. The silence of a dark pool is evidence of an unearthly presence. On the wider field of an evening landscape the stillness is felt as the very presence of God.

Music, stillness, dream: these are elements of the poet's world which tune his spirit to Reality. Of a different order is love. Without love the human soul is utterly incapacitated from even recognizing the possibility of the existence of Reality, much more of diagnosing its nature; so the poet's soul is superlatively rich in love. What he loves he loves "past words to tell". His love, his praise, his gratitude "for everything" to the lord of the "pined for Spring" are too deep for utterance. Love does not lose its urgency as the years pass—"All that I love I love anew now parting draweth near". With him love's prayer has a strange potency, turning grief into flowers, unkindness into the calling of cool water, blindness to beauty into loving-kindness. Personal love, the love between man and woman, the love of children, has amazing, vital, electric effects on the poet's mind, making it godlike. Love brings ineffable peace. Though life turn to ashes, forgetfulness is found in love's simplicity; hope may go but love is undying. Love is supreme: love's lightest word has the significance of thunder; love is changeless as the heavens, and sets the stars alight. Even love's sorrow is divine, terrible but sweet and uplifting; the memory of a lost love makes of night a thing of endless wonder and beauty. The uttermost, the undiscoverable secret belongs to love and silence: there is a soundless fount of knowledge and song hidden in some dark place of the imagination where divine Silence keeps perpetual vigil and timeless Love broods like the Phoenix.

The poet is newly assured of the spiritual nature of the real world by a feeling that in that world the spirits of the dead continue to exist. He has been aware of a brooding hush which encompassed two friends and, "stooping near", was intent to hearken their lightest words; at another time of something "less even than a shadow" that leaned above a mother and listened to the words of a story she read only (as she supposed) to her children. He feels the real presence of a lost beloved haunting his solitude. Indeed, there is nothing more urgent, actual, real, in the whole of de la Mare's experience than the ghost-presences adumbrated in such poems as *Faithless*, *Vigil*, *The Vision* and *The Ghost* (a) and (b). There have been moments when a strange, sweet, ominous impulse of happiness has welled up in his soul and sunk back again; and he explains such exquisite spiritual sensations as speechless messages of a ghost to his inward ear;* he regrets only that his senses, delicate

---

* These impulses, sensations, which are not confined to poets, are amongst the most vivid and memorable of experiences: in another poem, *Mist*, de la Mare calls them "miracles of sunshine" breaking into his solitude, and accounts for the "secret influence" by asking, "Has then the mind no inward sun?"

and subtle as they are, yet fail to understand the significance of those messages. Just so he knows there are voices calling "come" by the river, spirits that wander in the meadows and touch the cheeks of children, watchers in the twilight—but even he cannot tell us who they are. What he has learnt is that on those occasions, so rare and so elusive, when the spirits speak to us it is with courtesy and love, and that they are happily interested in mortals—perhaps each of us has a "familiar", the wraith of a shadow, who forms our private link with the unseen. He knows too that at any moment a great angel may come flaming through the world, seen by none but frightened but not incredulous children.

Indeed it is to the credulity, or simple faith, of childhood that the poet owes most of his knowledge of the supernal world. To me, whose sensible contacts with spiritual reality have come entirely in later life, this inversion of the natural processes of mental growth seems in itself a fairy tale, but those poets, like Vaughan and Wordsworth, who bear witness in the matter are agreed in their support of de la Mare's experience of the "divine far hours of childhood". He feels that in the lonely dreams of a child there is a grace, a clarity, which are dulled to extinction by the growth of worldly wisdom. He instances—perhaps in contrast to Wordsworth's heart that leaped up—the serene smiling acceptance by a child, reading by a stream, of a rainbow so splendid that at its sight "twice ten thousand warriors" might have cracked the firmament with their shouted joy. He commends the recluse who died, as he had lived, a child, for he believes that the human spirit is not free until it has learnt to be "with self reconciled", and that this can be done only by "retrieving the wisdom I lost as a child". There was a Sabbath peace, a respite safe from trouble, in certain childhood moments, and the memory of them has a mystic value. A poem of extraordinary power and loveliness tells how the dream of absolute beauty, present to the child, departed at the moment when the "child's heart woke from sleep". The world is still marvellously beautiful, but that supreme vision will never come again, though the poet's heart, and with it all nature, yearns but to catch its fleeting foot. He has two gleams of comfort: the secret, though untold, is half-divulged—*es leuchtet mir ein*, as Teufelsdröckh cried; and though all else come to naught, that once-seen absolute beauty cannot die, nor the quest of it cease.

> Only thou immortally
>   Hauntest on
> This poor earth in Time's flux caught;
> Hauntest on, pursued, unwon,
> Phantom child of memory,
> Beauteous one!*

* It will be observed that this poem, *The Phantom* (b), is a dellamarian version of the *Immortality Ode*. Apart from a few slight verbal parallels the poem enters into no rivalry with Wordsworth, but gives brief lyric expression to the theme which the *Ode* developed so definitively. In place of Wordsworth's huge intellectual grasp de la Mare's poem has a greater lyrical intensity: by the power of lyric form *The Phantom* achieves within its slender compass an effect equal to that of the slowly accumulated force of the tremendous *Ode*. It is interesting to notice that both poems were composed

The Poetry of Reality

The poet is confirmed in his belief in the existence of the world of spirit by his equally strong apprehension of the unreality of the world of sense. "All I love in beauty cries to me, 'We but vain shadows and reflections be' ". However sweet and insistent the world of sense may be, it but "feigns Reality", and must "resign to cloaked Eternity" something which man's spirit, a stranger upon earth, perceives from the vantage ground of dream. This world we walk in has a dream-like quality: sometimes in the silvery dawn "the enormous earth lies like a dream outspread"; in the presence of some still and lovely scene the thought may come that the place is but the dream of a distant dreamer. A tranquil voice and a loved personality can dissolve the present and transform time. The effect of the grace and joy of a bird is such that it seems that the leafy world is part of the bird's life, and might at any moment "vanish in song".

Life to the poet is so full of marvel and magic that he questions its substantiality, and perceives that it is an emanation from some deeper life. As evening comes down, the fields are no longer man's but are filled with the mystery of God. Night, with its silence and its eerie sounds beneath the starlit heavens, brims with magic. The growing plant and the climbing wave are a constant miracle; the simplest things, the humblest creatures, of nature may be invested with a light of eternity. There are things "usual yet miracu-

---

while their writers were in the early thirties. The *Ode* is more positive on what remains—those "high instincts" which the later years can never "utterly abolish and destroy". This stage of thought is suggested by de la Mare in *Arabia*, written a little later.

60

lous" out of which comes a sense that blesses the feeling heart. The loveliness of a chance-seen face "hovers a mystery between dream and real". Chance is itself so strange, so provocative of question: the accidental meeting—perhaps in a railway carriage— of people who will never meet again, or the separating of tracks and lives to different destinies. How great is the miracle of a universe passing through the minute window of the human eye. Every time we sleep it is to miracle and wonder that we wake; courage sees life as a wondrous thing even in the blind hour of stress. The stuff of life, magic-woven and rich of hue, is too often wasted in pursuits and thoughts trivial, sordid, ugly: Queen Djenira and the Dark Château and the King of Never to Be show what fascinating things the creative mind can make from it. The poet defines the world and himself in a phrase—

the world whose wonder
Was the very proof of me,

and calls upon the self to awake and find "all Heaven around thee".

Man himself—his life and his mind—even on the plane of everyday existence, is so entirely wonderful that he is only explicable in the light of a hypothesis of something more wonderful still. How mysterious is the self, how subtle the relationship of one self to another; what poetry is to be found in personality; how incomprehensible are suffering and happiness. Memory is an angel, fantasy the gift of the gods, genius the god himself. Thought can immortalize a

61

vanishing loveliness. The self, maroooned on the island of life, is the source of all knowledge, and the deepest wisdom comes from the heart. The mind can steep itself in enchantment, and so touch strange states of being which may be symbols of eternity. Though compassed in mystery and peril and bound by an iron law, man's spirit is unquenched because its fire is

> Blown to a core of ardour
> By the awful breath of God.

The sense of wonder attaches with peculiar force to nature: it rises, an afflatus, from that spirit of nature which Wordsworth made his own. As the poet of *The Prelude* stood

> Beneath some rock, listening to sounds that are
> The ghostly language of the ancient earth,
> Or make their dim abode in distant winds,

so for de la Mare the wandering wind and the dark breakers beating on the shore "ever call to the lone ghost" in him, making him homesick, wasted with "vain and unassuageable desire". The simpler sounds of nature may convey their own significance: the tapping of a bird at a window may portend the coming of a spirit, the calling of an owl hints at far mysteries, the lapwing's anguished cry disturbs the soul. There is something mystical in the contemplative peace brought by the tranquil loveliness of England's hills and valleys, woods and breaking seas. Pan is not dead, but still "sings sweet out of earth's fragrant shade", and leaves among the violets "tears of an antique bitterness".

Last, but not least potent, of the evidences of a spiritual reality is beauty. When Keats said (or made the Greek Urn say) "Beauty is truth", he meant that beauty is the stamp of eternity upon time. Though earthly beauty is but transient, and the happiness it brings is breathed upon a sigh, man feels that his home, the peace of his spirit, is with the eternal beauty, and he, or the poet in him, must follow the lure of beauty to the world's end. Some ineffable loveliness was lost when man's spirit came from "far Arabia" to "this haunt of brooding dust", but it is vividly recalled by the beauty of earth, and man's life is shadowed by a dream. For beauty is a secret dream, and few can know her: if one who has grown earth-bound should come to take beauty by chance he must let her go—she is not for him. For the others, for the few· wiser or more fortunate, a clear vision of starry loveliness is, even unto death, the steadfast desire of the soul's loyalty. Love itself may be the memory of a lost vision of spiritual beauty. For there are two beauties, of earth and of spirit: earthly beauty is entrancing, but it fades in ashes, and the Wanderer turn his back upon it to follow the spiritual beauty. Beauty herself is immortal, one of three immortalities: God, and God's creations, man and beauty.

The poet, as artist, provides us with the sources of delight, the subtle delight which we cannot describe but call aesthetic. This is his primary function, and if he fulfils it adequately we have no complaint to bring against him. But the great poets are not only artists, but share with inspired religious teachers the privilege of being the vehicles of God, the power to convince us of life's part in the scheme of eternity. Milton does this directly by giving aesthetic passion to the religious sense; Shakespeare does it by investing human fate, human relations, and especially human speech with a grandeur that places them in the category of the immortal; Wordsworth by his mystic sense of God in nature; Shelley by his exaltation of universal love; Keats and Tennyson by their apprehension of the miracle of beauty; Arnold and Hardy by their high sense of the pathos of the human situation. De la Mare is a member of this order of poets by reason of his perception that everything human is a shadow cast by something eternal. It is, I think, impossible to read extensively in de la Mare without realizing that life's beauty and mystery are a foreshowing of a life immeasurably more beautiful and mysterious, a life immortal and divine—that earthly life is a faint thin pattern of the life of God.

Note. I have wished to avoid interrupting the text of this chapter with footnotes giving titles of poems, but the substance of the chapter is based upon the undermentioned poems in the order given.

The Listeners	The Familiar	Memory (a)
The Traveller	Tom's Angel	Fog
The Glimpse	Rooks in October	To K.M.
Sleep	Dreams (a)	When the Rose is
The Stranger (d)	The Rainbow (b)	Faded
The Three Strangers	A Sunday	The Candle
The Catechism	The Phantom (b)	A Song of Enchant-
A Portrait (b)	Thou art my Long	ment
Music (a)	Lost Peace	The Children of
A Song of Shadows	Dawn	Stare

64

The Visionary World

The Sleeper (a)	The Sunken Garden	Homesick
Swallows Flown	Martha	The Tomtit
The Creek	The Linnet	The Owl (c)
Evening (a)	Evening (a)	These Solemn Hills
A Portrait (b)	Night (a)	England
Dust	The Miracle	Sorcery
For All the Grief	Old Shellover	They Told Me
The Ghost (a)	A Portrait (b)	Quiet Enemy
Vigil	The Railway Junction	Snow (b)
The Ghost (b)	The Window (b)	Vain Questioning
The Remonstrance	The Sleeper (b)	The Decoy
Invocation	Courage	Arabia
Autumn	Fare Well	Music (a)
Remembrance	Awake	The Song of the
Winter Dusk	The Slum Child	Secret
Faithless	Mercutio	The Old Angler
Solitude	The Veil	The Vision
Voices	A Young Girl	The Visionary
The Three Strangers	Pollie	The Journey
The Wanderer	The Widow	The Scribe

(NOTE. Each of the three columns should be read continuously.)

CHAPTER V

Theotherworlde

THE spiritual world we have been considering is of terrific seriousness: the frequency and conviction of his intimations of that world are the measure of a poet's ultimate importance. One of those "intimations" we have found to be the poet's impression of the unreality and unpredictableness of the tangible world. But this world, solid and actual, yet perceived as faintly unreal, and interpenetrated by magic—the otherworlde of *Come Hither*, or what Lord Dunsany calls "the haunted land of de la Mare" —may be appreciated disinterestedly, enjoyed for its own fascinating sake. It is the land of fantasy, lying half-way between actuality and reality. Most people, .other than a few very superior persons and such as are depressed or dulled by long addiction to the study of science, delight in gramarye. They may not think it matters much, but they are willing to lose themselves for awhile in this delightful garden.

Occasionally a keeper comes along and orders them out. Mr. I. A. Richards, in his provocative little book, *Science and Poetry*, declares that nature has been so completely "neutralized" by the scientific attitude that no trace of magic remains: he predicts from this the death of poetry. His conclusion has some plausibility (in the light of modern tendencies in verse), but his reasoning seems at fault: the demise of poetry may be imminent, but not from this cause.

Apart from the fact that there are themes and sources of poetry outside "nature"; apart also from the "suspicion" of a celebrated scientist that the universe is "not only queerer than we suppose but queerer than we *can* suppose"; there are even yet whole provinces of the supernatural quite unaffected, for the ordinary man and the ordinary poet, by the explanations of science. The day is far distant when psycho-analysis shall have robbed of its allure the incalculable world of dreams. Imaginative people will remain for whom certain states, such as love or silence, will always induce the supernatural; others for whom a light of unreality always plays over "real" things. Small children and small animals are so utterly different from human nature as adults understand it that they belong to another world: for all we know they are as near the fairies as they seem to be. Inanimate nature itself, however well known to be the product of forces more or less understood, has a habit of silencing our condescending expositions with a gesture of strangeness.

Just when we're safest, there's a sunset touch,
A fancy from a flower-bell. . . .

Nature has pantheistic moods of her own, and they are not to be denied at the bidding of science. So at least thinks de la Mare, and with him some other major writers of the last half century whose imagination draws sustenance from the supernatural—Yeats, Barrie, Kipling, Mr. James Stephens, Lord Dunsany.

To see in poetry of this kind nothing but pretty fancies, fit to charm an idle hour but worthless as a criticism of life, is to ignore that half of life which is crammed with the inexplicable. Everything perhaps has its cause (though even physics has lately admitted passing doubts about this), but if the cause is an infinitely complex one, made up of a myriad interacting causes, most of them unknown to us, meeting in one event, things might as well have no cause at all, or a "supernatural" one. It is not a matter of argument and proof. What are called "religious experiences" can be explained away as normal psychological processes, but the man who has had the experience smiles at such explanations: he says he "knows", and the meaning of life is changed for him. So too with magic experience: once meet it full, or even grasp its inherent likelihood fully with your imagination, and, science notwithstanding, the world becomes a marvellous and exciting place where anything may happen; and of this unpredictable world de la Mare is the critic, the interpreter, the priest and the poet. No one so completely unites both sides of the lyrical Ballads formula: for him, and for his readers, the "natural" world is alive with the supernatural, the supernatural world is as vitally present as the world of sense. Dr. Susan Stebbing (*Philosophy and the Scientists*) suggests that spread over the scientist's clearly defined world of universal causation are two "films of negligible haziness"—the system of the atom, and the human mind. Why should not magic form a third such film?* Life is an iridescent bubble of magic blown on the

* It may be that only the atomic film belongs to Dr. Stebbing, and that the second, like the third, is my deduction from her argument.

68

breath of reality; and which is of first importance, the air that supports the unsubstantial envelope or the envelope that encloses the yet more unsubstantial air, who shall say?

Doubtless this conception of things, this reaction to life, is primitive, irrational, childlike. De la Mare cheerfully accepts the epithets. The world he apprehends is not infrequently described as a dream-world, but the term implies a certain scepticism in those who use it. I prefer to see in de la Mare's faculty a more intense wakefulness, an awareness tuned to a higher pitch than the normal, so that things and experiences which hover beyond the limits of our apprehension are within the circle of his, and are communicated to us in his poetry. It may well be that such communications of such experiences will not bear analysis suitable to conceptions of a more rational order, but they should take no harm from sympathetic description.

Ghosts are not to be considered here. As we have seen, and as we shall see again, ghosts have a special place and significance in de la Mare's poetry. Far from being "unreal", they are a part of reality itself. For the purpose of this chapter we have come out of eternity into the common air. But it is common air effervescent with the incredible: life on the human plane, and yet life seen through the crystal of de la Mare's bizarre mind. To de la Mare it seems unlikely that those characteristics of mortal life which appeal most to him—its waywardness and humour, its charm and its malice, its love of mystification—are mere subjective illusions. All the sub-human world,

69

too, probably has a hidden life of its own, whose rare impingements upon our awareness strike us as alien, supernatural. People who put their faith in mechanical speed and industrial progress are totally insensitive to these contacts, but many children and some adults are uncorrupted, and for them the poems and stories of de la Mare are rich in otherworldly treasure.

Fairies, witches and ogres are there chiefly to please the children (except the allegorical witch of *The Journey*), but only the grimmest grown-up will refuse to accept the charming fairy who gives old Sam Shore three wishes, in a poem which is perhaps just a fantastic trifle, but is, perhaps again, one of the memorable poems of our time. Whether we think of Sam's second life as a dream between two taps at the door, or as a real magic miracle, the imaginative vision of "life's little whirligig" is in the tradition of great poetry. Another and more sophisticated Sam, who lived by the sea, tells with convincing detail how he was tempted by a mermaid. And there are some lovely naiads, though the most realistic of them is a symbol of beauty, and belongs to the world of the previous chapter. There are other fairies, among them a mocking fairy whom Charles Williams found "dreadful", and some fairy children, notably the changeling at whose beauty the young ferryman fell into a dream and so drifted, stern-foremost, down, down to the sea. There is a realistic Ogre (too realistic for tender-minded parents) whom the name of Jesus only just stopped from eating two sleeping children in Trebarwith Vale:

Into their dreams no shadow fell
Of his disastrous thumb
Groping discreet and gradual
Across the quiet room.

And the Pedlar in the poem of that name comes from some other and sinister world.

"Pluck not a hair!" a hidden rabbit cried,
"With but one hair he'll steal thy heart away,
Then only sorrow shall thy lattice hide:
Go in! all honest pedlars come by day."
There was dead silence in the drowsy wood;
"Here's syrup for to lull sweet maids to sleep,
And bells for dreams, and fairy wine and food. . . ."

I have already said something of the marvellous way in which "form" is employed in this poem for the "suspension of disbelief", effecting its purpose more successfully, I think, than do the humour and descriptive force of *Goblin Market*. The art of the poem is perfect, and the wonder is that such art and such passionate rhythm should be lavished on so slight a theme. Not that the theme remains slight when so treated: the poem becomes so clearly one of high seriousness that the reader may be tempted to see some allegory in the tale of Lettice and her lock of hair, but will be wise to avoid any but the vaguest suggestion of such. Perhaps a vision of "a malady most incident to maids"; otherwise just a study in the not impossible.

There are poems that embody the "real supernatural", the strange and disturbing experiences that

71

come to some people more readily than to others. *The Listeners* (though essentially a "visionary" poem*) may be read in this way. One can avoid "explanation" of any sort: it remains a wonderful poem even if one gives every word its literal meaning and asks no questions. It may be regarded as a rendering, subtly heightened, of the always uncanny experience of an approach to an empty and long-deserted house. But for most people the poem is an interpretation of the feeling that one is "moving about in worlds not realized". One knocks—wonders —questions: but no one answers or descends; one listens: and knows only that one is surrounded by a host of phantom listeners; sometimes one even feels "the one man left alive". Such feelings may mean much or little to us, but man cannot live by science and economics alone, by what Wordsworth calls "the vulgar light of present actual superficial life". Hence for some of us—especially where those three magicians, nature, art and time have been at work, as in a "sunken garden"—marvellous possibilities are never far off:

> Breathe not—trespass not;
> Of this green and darkling spot,
> Latticed from the moon's beams,
> Perchance a distant dreamer dreams;

(not impossible, but quite without significance, says matter-of-fact)—

---

* A special significance attaches to this poem as the first of the three poems Thomas Hardy asked his wife to read to him as he lay on his death-bed.

Theotherworlde

Perchance upon its darkening air
The unseen ghosts of children fare,
Faintly swinging, sway and sweep
Like lovely sea-flowers in its deep;

(interesting, if true, says matter-of-fact, but there is
no measurable evidence of its being true).

The comments overlook the fact that much of life
rests on illusion, and that it is often impossible to
separate the illusory from the actual; whence it follows that there is no more reason why we should culti-
vate and attend to what most people have agreed to
call actual than to what most people take to be
illusion. Correspondence with mood is a species of
truth, and for a certain mood it may be true to say that

An ominous bird sang from its branch
Beware, O Wanderer!

The childish fancy that there is "someone" in the
orchard or at the window leads directly on to the
mature feeling, rich in value, of the poet as he sits
alone and happy and knows suddenly that a joy has
gone out of the sunshine—

A presence my mood estranged
Went grieved away;

or at another time realizes that the solitude is "mute
with a presence unearthly fair".

Life is endlessly interesting, take it how you will,
but this sense of the supernatural doubles the interest.
It has other reactions than those touched upon. It

may throw an aspect of the mysterious over "ordinary" things, leaving them none the less part of the workaday scheme. Thus in *The Sleeper* the situation of a girl finding her mother asleep is seen in a new dimension, and made rich and strange. The poet's unequalled power of creating stillness and tranquillity is put forth through the simple rhythm and an exquisite choice of words, but the magic of the house filled with sleep, and the girl's cloud-like dread—these things have been felt and known, and are now part of experience for us as well as the poet. Some of his women—Caroline, Sophia, Sephina—though engaged in the ordinary doings of life, are transfigured with a light of enchantment, removed, fixed for ever in "the other world" of some still, rich, "waxen" interior.

I watched the Lady Caroline
      Bind up her dark and beauteous hair;
Her face was rosy in the glass
And, 'twixt the coils, her hands would pass
      White in the candle-shine. . . .

The snowy light lay dim without,
      I heard the waits their sweet song sing,
The window smouldered keen with frost,
Yet still she twisted, sleeked and tossed
      Her beauteous hair about.

More often, however, de la Mare takes the next step and carries us into a world which, though geographically mundane, is not otherwise recognizable as the daily scene. It is here that his prose most obviously aligns with his poetry, for much of the prose

74

is of this border-line supernatural order. His far lands, his Tartary, his Arabia, are flooded with un- earthly light, there are nameless other-world places recalling those tantalizing cities of our dreams that haunt our waking with memories more vivid than those of our native town. Think once more of that still, turreted house with moonlit door to which the Traveller first came knocking: in spite of its specious links with the natural world—its leaf-fringed sill, the turf and the ferny floor of the forest—it is no mortal habitation, will never come into .the hands of the National Trust or be scheduled as an Ancient Monu- ment: the silence that surged softly backward when the plunging hoofs were gone will never again be broken. Hardly less unearthly is the stone house named "Alas", the dwelling-place of those heedless children of the gods who must each at length alone pass out of its beauty into the starlit night, "con- fronted" as they do so (and this is not its least un- earthly feature) by that worn "Alas" writ plain above the portal. Or there is that Valley with its Tower of Ivory,* now rotting with age and weakness, and looking out over a shoreless sea; or the dark château, confessedly built by dream-hands high above the dream-waters of a far ravine; or the realm of the childless King of Never-to-be. Where is the garden of the three cherry trees in which the ghost of the happy and beautiful lady wanders; or the graveyard where the listening cherub's head keeps its secret; or

* This poem, *Time Passes*, is doubtless an allegory of the in- dividual life from childhood to age, just as the poem of the house "Alas" (*The Dwelling-place*) is an allegory of the life of mankind.

75

The Poetry of Reality

where are the courts of the Lord Pthamasar wherein
Queen Djenira walks? It is with these places as with
"the icy hills with frosty ulys overgrown"—

Yea, in my mind these mountains rise—

and the strange uncharted globe of de la Mare's mind
hangs in the sky of poetry with light no less lovely
than that of the moon herself.

In *The Traveller* it is nothing less than the whole
round earth that is taken up into the poet's imaginative vision and transmuted into pure de la Mare. This
long and delightful poem is a story of enthralling
interest set in a landscape brilliantly imagined and
visualized, with a philosophic hero riding a most
lovable Arab mare. The conception underlying the
tale, that the earth is a sentient being, with an "eye"—
which is the same as saying that the earth is the eye of
the universe—accords well with modern views of life
and evolution, matter and spirit. The working out of
the idea—the traveller's ride over a huge, gently-
curving plateau, a convex of coloured rock, which at
first shows "branched veins of sanguine in a milk-pale
stone", but as he proceeds lapses into a blue "divine
as Eros' eyes", a vitreous region, "like a sea asleep,
crystalline, convex, tideless and congealed", until at
the summit he finds himself looking down into "an
immeasurable well of lustrous crystal, motionlessly
black", out of which there gazes "a presence": this
presentation of Earth's eye may seem a little too concrete for some tastes, but in the poem itself, as distinct
from a summary, the detail is lightly stressed and un-

76

disturbing (indeed the critics who reviewed the poem on its first appearance did not seem to have noticed the "eye" at all, in spite of the "concentric shadows" and the three areas of "white", "iris" and "pupil")* The traveller is something more than that figure of romance, the Solitary Horseman: he must be taken for what he is—"one who explores pure fantasy's unbounded realm": who else but the poet? He attains "the true intent of his unbroken pilgrimage"; he has perceived a consciousness in the world of matter, "rapt, immaterial, remote". He feels that he is no despairing castaway, but an explorer of the infinite, eager to achieve Life's kiss of rapture. And so he comes to his fathomless well of truth, dies at this "moment of desire", and the mare gallops off in panic.

Life to de la Mare is "a strange city". He is "lost in Paradise". He feels an exile, "whose every exiled day gone by aches" with the memory of the gods who loved him not. It is inadequate to say that he "fails to distinguish between the two worlds, real and unreal". There are not two such worlds. There is one world, but two ways of experiencing it, which are indeed so different that they seem to present two worlds: the world of the commonplace imposed upon us by the routine of civilization, and the world of free experience, which, whether actual or occult, material or

* It may be that the critics do not accept my gloss. This, rather than discourtesy, may be the explanation of why the T.L.S. did not publish my letter drawing attention to the failure of all the reviewers to mention this feature of the poem. I should doubtless have been no more acute than other readers but for a hint I received from the poet himself a year or so before *The Traveller* appeared.

77

imaginative, is for ever unique, unpredictable, incredible: at one time "eternity ... like a great ring
of pure and endless light", at another, "the last red
leaf ... on the topmost bough that looks up at the
sky". All experience is equally "real", but that which
has become commonplace has ceased to have significance. The ratio of one kind of experience to the
other differs from man to man; de la Mare has re-
duced his commonplace world to zero. All life for
him has value, and a meaning beyond itself. His
music, all his sounds, are echoes, his people are
ghosts—

> your ghostly lips and eyes
> Made wisdom unwise ... O vision grave.

Martha was actual enough to "sit with her two slim
hands clasped round her bended knees", yet as her
stories unfolded

> Fairies and gnomes stole out
> In the leaf-green light,
>
> And her beauty far away
> Would fade, as her voice ran on,
> Till hazel and summer sun
> And all were gone.

Sleep, as a lesser death, has for all poets something
of mystery and provocativeness, and de la Mare has
told us (in *Behold This Dreamer* and elsewhere) how
endlessly interesting he finds its enigma. He almost
fears to think how men "commit themselves to sleep".
He is exercised by the problem of where the mind and

spirit go when the body is asleep. (Where do you go when your car runs out of petrol on a country road?) He feels there is a kind of romantic beauty in just sitting alone in the dark: to do so brings refreshment to the spirit as cool water to the body.

Dreams, I am inclined to think (and have suggested in the somewhat frivolous parenthesis occurring a few lines back), belong to theotherworlde rather than to the world of spiritual vision, but de la Mare takes them more seriously, as well he may, in view of the marvellous nature of his dreams, as narrated in some of his poems and in the introduction to that noble collection, *Behold This Dreamer*. (We all get the dreams we deserve.) He enjoys watching the operation of the mind in sleep and (especially) half-sleep: he sees that in these conditions the mind is not under control but thinks and imagines freely, bringing to its "owner" things unsought. The long poem called *Dreams* (b) is a reasoned defence of dreaming, showing its joys, terrors, and interest: it declares that much of life is a dream, and that the waking and the dream worlds are inextricably mixed. The last five stanzas state the conclusion of the whole matter. Knowledge is forlorn, is mere death, unless it is vitalized by imagination (dream); brain must be confirmed by heart and soul (Wordsworth's "feeling intellect"). Imagination is the feminine complement of reason, and Eden was empty till Adam dreamed Eve. So creative is dream, for in dreams the "timeless self" beats against the prisoning walls, and the night that brings no dream is wasted. From dream de la Mare has learnt that the need of the soul is "energy in

79

peace" whereby man shall be "at one with nature's mystery", so that he can "seek love beneath the tree of life". This is "profound thinking" indeed, and provides ample justification for de la Mare's preoccupation with "the dream of sleep".

But after all, the true home of the supernatural, of theotherworlde, is nature. Other aspects can be explained away as emanations of an abnormal mind, but there remains the age-long sense of queer goings-on in that world of "inanimate" nature against the vast background of which man moves like a pygmy god. Originally a mere item in its multitudinousness, man has differentiated himself so thoroughly that nature and he are bitter enemies: he must enslave nature or nature will slay him. Perhaps the apparent hostility of nature (so convincing in Conrad's sea-pieces) is merely indifference: one feels it in the cold immensity of space, it is symbolized in the insect that crosses an arterial road unaware of any change that has come about since its progenitors crawled over the rocks of the pliocene. But, antagonism or unconcern,* the indisputable fact is the gulf of difference, a difference so complete as to produce in the imaginative mind an assured sense of magic in all the doings of nature. Nature is the great fairy.

Yet in truth, though this consciousness of natural magic informs all de la Mare's poetry, it becomes ex-

* To a disciple of Bergson and Shaw these are changed to timid friendship and tentative co-operation, blundering but honest; man is "one with nature", a living element in a homogeneous creative process. But such speculations are alien to de la Mare's way of thought.

plicit in only a limited number of his poems: he does not compare, in this respect, with the ancients or the Elizabethans, with Wordsworth, with W. H. Davies. The Greek sense of deity in nature is not very strong with him. *Nightfall* breathes pantheism:

> The coursers of the dark stamp down to drink,
> Arch their wild necks, lift their wild heads and neigh;
> Their drivers, gathering at the water-brink,
> With eyes ashine from out their clustering hair,
> Utter their hollow speech. . . .
> Come the wood-nymphs to dance within the glooms,
> Calling these charioteers with timbrels' din. . . .
> And all the dwellers in the lonely know
> The unearthly are abroad. . . .

But as a rule he feels no need to be a pagan suckled in a creed outworn that nature may come alive for him. The hackneyed miracle of growth is still the miracle it was to Adam:

> Who beckons the green ivy up
> Its solitary tower of stone?
> What spirit lures the bindweed's cup
>   Unfaltering on?
> Calls even the starry lichen to climb
> By agelong inches endless Time?

The moon, which in *Peacock Pie*, was merely though marvellously beautiful, walking the night in her silver shoon, has in *Motley* become a potency, able to make lovers wise and to flood their secret world with her twilight, while in *The Burning-glass* she is the deity of that "still and starry mystery", the dark garden which occupies one half of the poet's mind. Some of de la Mare's woods are almost as magic as the Woods of Westermain—

> A song of Enchantment I sang me there
> In a green-green wood by waters fair;

and there is a dim leafy place lit by

> Elf-light, bat-light,
> Touchwood-light and toad-light,
> And the sea a glimmering gloom of grey.

There are those other "very old" woods, with buds so old with their beauty that they carry man back to Solomon and Eden. The landscape of *Remembrance* is full of magic—

> Lofty and few the elms, the stars
>   In the vast boughs most bright;
> I stood a dreamer in a dream
>   In the unstirring night.

So is that of *The Phantom* (b)—

> Utter quiet falls; the wind
>   Sighs no more.
> Yet it seems the silence yearns. . . .

In poems of *The Burning-glass* the moon is spectral as the dingles of the woodland listen to the owl's ahooh; the dove-like tenderness of a February sky hints at hidden mysteries; a lonely lane emerging on a sea-cliff cries a challenge to the trespasser.

When we come to those queer links between man and inanimate nature, the animals, we have already agreed to include with them—children. De la Mare specializes in subhuman creatures: fairies, Mulla-Mulgars, animals, midgets, children. The classification is sound. The nearest equivalent to fairies we can get in the objective world are small animals and birds, and children between, say, two years old and ten (babies are all too human in spite of a certain gnomishness, but you may extend my figures a little down if you like, and, for girls, up to twelve or thirteen). As for the smaller creatures of the wild (and with them the kitten of the domestic cat, and perhaps the cat herself, but not dogs—not even puppies, which are as human as babies), if these are not fairies, what are they? When Puck and Peaseblossom lose their spell, the enchantment of the ousel-cock, the throstle and the wren with little quill is as strong as ever. The poet sees fairies dancing in a ring, and hears a linnet singing near: the fairies fade all too soon but the linnet's song goes on. At a flutter of a bird's wing the landscape may dissolve, vanish in song—a possibility on the brink of which the natural world in de la Mare constantly hovers. There is the old witch-hare that fled like a ghostie leaving only the moonlight behind; and there is that immortal trio of nocturnal adventurers, Shellover, Creep and Sallie Worm, baptised into faerie by dew and the light of the rising moon.

Children are of course important in de la Mare's

poetry for other reasons than their fairy-like quality, but no other poet has so convincingly demonstrated that children are akin to fairies, to animals, to the spirit-world—to anything rather than to adult humans. How instant and perfect is the sympathy between the child and the ghost-child in *The Phantom* (a). How completely unsurprised is little Louisa when, sitting by her bedroom window in the early morning,

> She slanted her small bead-brown eyes
> Across the empty street,
> And saw Death softly watching her
> In the sunshine pale and sweet

The simple recognition of a creature akin to herself passes to curiosity: she "peeps small" at him, and when he wags a little key at her goes quietly down to him. One's heart stands still, but she discovers the illusion, and is no more surprised at that. Only

> she thought how strange it was
> Two keys that he should bear,
> And that, when beckoning, he should wag
> The littlest in the air.

The child's attitude towards death as a concrete fact—expressed with characteristic naïveté by Wordsworth in *We Are Seven* and with characteristic savagery by Hardy in *Mother Won't Know*—is shown in all its detached but charming inhumanity in *The Funeral*, where the children, "Susan and Tom and Me", ignore altogether the occasion for their being "dressed

84

up in black", and are engaged solely with trees,
flowers, birds and the wind in Susan's hair, and afterwards tea in the nursery and the thrushes singing out
of window while Tom falls asleep in his chair—"He
was so tired, poor thing." De la Mare's children are
anything but little men and women. Sometimes they
are bird-like, as in *The Thief at Robin's Castle*, or in the
poem about the housewarming—

> And when all the guests were gone, and
> All was still as still can be,
> In from the dark ivy hopped a
> Wee small bird: and that was me;

sometimes moon-like—

> So, for a while, each gazed at each,
> Dick and the solemn moon.

The boy and the donkey understand each other like
lovers:

> And over the grass would seem to pass,
> 'Neath the deep dark blue of the sky,
> Something much better than words between me
> And Nicholas Nye.

It is in this personal, intimate way of magic and
humour that de la Mare "goes" (as Tagore says of
Wordsworth) "to meet nature" (and other forms of
non-human existence) "with imagination". The
classical approach he leaves to Flecker—

> Though I was born a Londoner
> And bred in Gloucestershire,
> I walked in Hellas years ago. . . .

The Poetry of Reality

Have I not chased the fluting Pan
Through Cranham's sober trees?
Have I not sat on Painswick Hill
With a nymph upon my knees,
And she as rosy as the dawn
And naked as the breeze?

De la Mare is rather of the mind of Rupert Brooke—

Some it may be . . . have seen
A Faun a-peeping through the green . . .
Or heard the Goat-foot piping low:
But these are things I do not know.
I only know. . . .

It is an English, or a Teutonic, sense. It is simple and
direct, perhaps it is sentimental; it is the way of pure
feeling and love, an entering into the life of nature and
into nature's secrets with enjoyment, sympathy, self-
surrender. It is a way that commends itself to the
modern mind because of its directness of contact. It
rests on no assumptions, it offers no explanations, it
draws no inferences, moral or other. It is the negation
of materialism, yet never loses touch with phenomena;
it is subjective, but minutely faithful to fact. The world
is photographed on the delicate sensitivity of de la
Mare's mind, and the picture that comes out shows,
standing behind the world's shoulder, the ghost of
theotherworlde.

CHAPTER VI

This World

THE claim has been made for de la Mare that,
even when most preoccupied with faerie, he
walks on common earth, that among his ghosts
there strays the reassuring donkey. Small comfort,
however, for those who fear the dark, in an animal
whose mortality no one can with certainty affirm; and
Nicholas Nye, the only donkey I can find in de la
Mare, is a moonshiny ethereal beast. There are pigs,
too, but they are but part of the charcoal-burner's
dream, if indeed both he and they are not thoughts in
the mind of night as she walks her starry ways. He
has a few "real" people, three-dimensional and individual, like Old Susan and Old Ben, Miss Loo and
the Fat Woman, but the great majority of his people
—Martha, Sephina, Ann and her mother, the Old
Angler, the Lovely, the Sabbath child, K.M., the
Blind Boy—are fairies, just as much as the witch-hare
and the dog with the silver paws.

The occasions on which de la Mare makes any
attempt to limn with the pencil of "fidelity to fact"
some "piece of life" are rare, and he generally has
some reason for leaving his native medium, just as
Shakespeare has when he turns from verse to prose.
Such simplicity as could only be spoilt by the further
simplification of fancy accounts for the examples
mentioned, as for *The Old Soldier* and *The Quar-
tette*—

87

The Poetry of Reality

Tom sang for joy and Ned sang for joy and old Sam sang
    for joy;
All we four boys piped up loud, just like one boy.

Humour generally demands some exactness of treatment, and in all the examples cited the picture is
treated with the observant eye of the humorist. De la
Mare's children are occasionally, under this condition, realistically observed. *Poor Henry* is certainly so
as he lifts distracted hands at sight and smell of the
physic that stands "thick in its glass", and scowls
when with a gurgle and a gasp it has gone down.
There is humour, as well as much else, in the deeply
etched picture of the children who were present in
body at *The Funeral* and so utterly far away in spirit.
Pity lends verisimilitude to the portraits of *Poor Miss* 7
and the old crone in *Age*, satire to that of the mother in
Reserved, and some blend of pity and satire to the
situation in *"Dry August Burned"*. And a new note in
observation faithfully recorded is struck in the exquisitely recognizable *Portrait* which stands at the
beginning of *The Burning-Glass*.

But de la Mare is the last poet who could be described as a poet of realism. His passionate and therefore poetic interest is almost entirely in that shadowy
provocative world which lies on the other side of
silence. As Mr. Shanks says, he is ever straining towards an unimaginable world more satisfactory than
the one that prisons him now. Earth itself he will not
accept—wishes it were "almost any other shape than
the shape it is", preferably "an infinite saucer", with
"ocean for ever pouring in enormous cataract into

space" over one edge. With what humorous sour distaste does he, in *Desert Islands*, epitomise the "scientific facts" about our world: "The earth, then, is a solid
steel-like orb—its mass, say, six thousand trillion
tons. It is so old that for several thousand million
years it has been capable of supporting "life". [One
remembers his own approach in *All That's Past.*] On
its extreme rind we humans crawl. It is rotating with a
(fortunately) unimaginable velocity; it is revolving—
"though proof of this is less simple"—round the sun;
it is so utterly isolated that, according to Sir James
Jeans, if, on self-extinction intent, it lay in wait in
space for a star to shatter it to less than atoms, its
suicidal suspense by the wayside might continue for
1,000,000,000,000,000,000 years. In spite of all
these noughts, could solitude be less eloquent? For
him, if the earth must be round (and he is quite un-
convinced on this point), he prefers, like his *Traveller*,
to think of it as "*un oeil énorme (qui) regarde la nuit*".

There is, however, one part of the sublunary order
that he unconditionally accepts, because it calls to the
depths of his spirit, and that is this island of England.
If "James Stephens has two loves, Ireland and
poetry", so likewise has Walter de la Mare—faerie
and England. Whenever beneath the shimmering
enchantment of his scene there seems to exist a basis
of substantial beauty lovingly observed with the
natural and naked eye, it is obviously a picture of
some piece of England. The linnet's dainty world of
bramble-spray and gold-wreathed furze, harebell and
thyme; the pastoral landscape of *Nod* and the ferny
woods of *The Listeners;* the grave of the beautiful lady

in the West Country; the quiet starred valley of *The Unchanging;* that inky tarn in thy hills (which should be Grisedale, but isn't, since de la Mare doesn't know the Lakes); the rusting harvest hedgerow entwined with Traveller's Joy: these are flying glimpses of the undying loveliness of England which keep breaking through to the rapt consciousness of the poet, and do not mar his vision.

Though his pages are peopled by ghosts and blown upon by winds from the unknown, they keep touch with normality through the frequent poems giving beautifully-noted fragments of the English scene. The pool to which *The Visionary* came, shadowed by the silver birch, is English in spite of—or because of —its mystery. The lovers in *The Tryst* (b) are heedless of ghosts but take care to tread softly, "Nor stir one England-wintering bird". *The English Downs* are here, with their lamb-besprinkled, green-turfed chalk. *Dawn* has its "old ashen rooks on ragged wing", its tinkling robin, its wool-fleeced ewes snuffing the morning air. Not only robins but wrens, tom-tits, owls, martins, swifts are everywhere, and the only sound among *These Solemn Hills* is "The lapwing's slow sad anguished *Pee-oo-eet*". There are flower studies, including of course the daisy, and a charming fancy that Rose Campion was sister to Thomas the poet-musician. If the thinning night-mists of *Sunrise* seem "Phantoms of beauty from a forgotten dream", *The Dreamer* himself kneels "in rusted coverts of the may" and listens through his dreams to the nightingale. For a world at peace the emblem is night o'er England and the air steeped in jasmine and honey-suckle. *A Sunday*—that exquisite poem of nostalgia for lost childhood—is quite obviously an English Sunday!

The natural scenery of one's native land is perhaps the only satisfactory basis for a perfectly pure patriotism. Military power, empire, pride of "race"—these are sources of hateful bastard patriotisms. But a love that in tenderness, intimacy, and purity from alien motives approaches the ideal love between man and wife is to be found, and found only, in the feeling that grows up in the heart of a man when for many years he has walked his country's ways, lived through her seasons with her, felt the lift of spirit as his eye has ranged over her loveliness in wood and water, hill and plain, and laid down stratum upon stratum of common memories. It is a patriotism easily consistent with Lowell's "patriotism of the soul". It is a love that is quite free from the adulteration of hate, for the lover of his country's beauty recognizes with genuine if condescending sympathy that the "foreigner" has every right to prefer the beauty of his own, and saves his dislike for those of his countrymen who seek a superficial and unsanctified pleasure in lands intended by nature for other men.

Such love of country is essentially, and in every sense, a thing of peace. It does not rise readily into the war-chant, and de la Mare's poetical response to the call of 1914 was scanty. *Motley*, published in 1918, fulfilled the demand to the extent of three poems. The first, *Happy England*, begins with the stiffness of an unnatural mode, but warms to the word England:

91

The Poetry of Reality

> Remember happy England: keep
> For her bright cause thy latest breath;
> Her peace that long hath lulled to sleep
> May now exact the sleep of death.
>
> Her woods and wilds, her loveliness. . . .

Another, *The Marionettes*, has a satiric power drawn from Hardy. The inter-War volumes contained a very few references to the past conflict, and the more recent struggle left just such slight impress—more deeply anguished but not more poetic—on *The Burning-glass*, published in 1945.

How can a poet write of England at war when to him England means peace? Fontenelle hated war because it spoiled conversation; de la Mare hates it because it poisons peace, the peace that is England. It was only when "the night-hawk's threat" and "the guns' low thunder" were gone that he could write lovingly,

> Night is o'er England. . . .
> Mysterious sleep has lulled her heart to rest,
> Deep even as theirs beneath her churchyard trees.

No land but England could give the peace from which his dream is born: the very word England spells peace in his ears. Nowhere, I think, does he use the colourless terms, Britain, Briton, British. (It would not be easy to say just why these terms seem alien to poetry, and call forth wrong responses. It can't be *only* because Tennyson claimed that God had set "His Briton" in blown seas.) But the singing vocables of

92

This World

"England" and "Englishman" carry their rich burden of dear significance through his pages: he loves to repeat them.

>Of all the trees in England,
>   Her three sweet corners in,
>Only the Ash, the bonny Ash,
>   Burns fierce when it is green.
>
>Of all the trees in England,
>   From sea to sea again,
>The Willow loveliest. . . .
>
>Of all the trees in England. . . .
>
>Of all the trees in England,
>   Oak, Elder, Elm and Thorn,
>The Yew alone burns lamps of peace
>   For them that lie forlorn.

The poem called *England* uses the beloved name only in the title, but lingers on all the things that make up the England of the poet's heart: her lovely hills that lay his tired thoughts to rest, the peace of her lovely valleys; the cool green refuge of her tranquil and dreamlike woods; her breaking seas that peal like trumpets; the clouds' bright towers of silence stealing into infinity. Nothing he has written has a more passionate sincerity than the last stanza of this poem:

>My heart within me faints to roam
>   In thought even far from thee:
>Thine be the grave whereto I come,
>   And thine my darkness be.

93

The Poetry of Reality

But the supreme, the simplest, expression of this feeling is *The Englishman*, a poem comparable in intensity with Henley's *England, my England*, and achieving its intensity without calling in "the song round the world on your bugles blown" or the "mailed hand" of the "Chosen daughter of the Lord". Here our representative Englishman is a characteristically dellamarian figure in a typically strange situation. Foreign-looking, with his long black hair, his shining blue eyes, and his silver ring, he has come "a-drifting landward on a spar" at dawn, and does not know what country it is on whose shores he has been "throwed up like corpses from the sea" within sight of his birthplace. Of the boy he meets in the woods he asks,

> What country, say, of this round earth,
>   What shore of what salt sea,
> Be this, my son, I wander in,
>   And looks so strange to me?

On being told he is in England,

> He lifts his voice yet louder,
>   What smell be this, says he,
> My nose on the sharp morning air
>   Snuffs up so greedily? . . .

> And oh, says he, what little bird
>   Is singing in yon high tree
> So every shrill and long-drawn note
>   Like bubbles breaks in me?

94

This World

At the truth he falls a-musing:

> England! he whispers, soft and harsh,
> England! repeated he,
> And briar and rose and mavis
> A-singing in yon high tree. . . .
>
> Ay, ay, I could not be mistook,
> I knew them leafy trees;
> I knew that land so witchery sweet
> And that old noise of seas.

There you have, instead of Henley's glib imperialism, the half-articulate feeling of the sailor, with his love breaking through in his whispered repetitions, his similes, his epithets—sharp, greedily, little, "that land so witchery sweet and that old noise of seas". The poet has chosen to include *The Englishman* with the *Rhymes and Verses*, but it is a deeply beautiful hymn of praise.

It is in the nature of things that de la Mare, who spends most of his time "abroad"—in theotherworlde —should, when he comes home, come home to England, to the England of Kipling's better mood:

> She is not any common earth,
> Water or sky or air,
> But Merlin's isle of gramarye.

This island England, secret as a College Quad by night, haunted by the myriad legends of her immemorial past, this Polyolbion of Drayton, Chaucer's "Lond fulfilled of faerie"—this island England

95

may well afford secure foothold for a poet whose eyes take in the far horizons of dreamland. For to love the English scene is to keep the mind sensitively attuned to that truth of magic which is as moonlight on the waters of phenomenal truth; and the spirit that leaps to meet the magic possibilities of life finds endless inspiration in the loveliness of England.

CHAPTER VII

Beauty

IT is not for nothing that the anthology which de la Mare made out of Nahum Tarune's three great volumes begins and closes with the timeless jingle which asserts, with duplicated emphasis and all the force of anonymity, the nature of "the key of the kingdom"—a basket of sweet flowers, symbol of beauty. Beauty is not "the kingdom" itself, nor even the door of the kingdom: the door by which the poet enters the kingdom is wonder, the visionary sense of eternal reality. It is perhaps only a matter of nomenclature. We have it on the authority of a great philosopher* that the teleology of the universe is directed to the production of beauty. If this were so (and belief is not difficult), beauty is the stuff of reality. But earthly beauty, the beauty which "moved away the pall from the dark spirit" of Keats, can be but the inchoate aspect of the beauty of the divine purpose, and for this a peculiarly apt figure is "the key", the mode of access between the visionary "kingdom" and the substantial world. With those other conceptions said to hold the secret of the universe—the mathematical one called "the square root of minus one" and the female human parallel one based on Shaw's inspired mistake, "the root of Myna's sex"—we may place the simplest and most perfect type of natural beauty, a flower. Beauty—flower-like, haunting,

*A. N. Whitehead, *Adventures of Ideas.*

97

miraculous—is the foot of the rainbow, whence the way into heaven is direct if difficult. The desire of de la Mare's soul is upward to where the rainbow leads; nevertheless he is with Wordsworth and Keats in passionate response to the present loveliness of earth, sea and sky.

The inspiration of de la Mare's feeling for nature has its source in light. His spirit goes out to atmospheric effects, the impeccable beauty of day—morning, noon and night and summer-evening. He watches with ecstasy the night-mists thin away as the sun rises through the gates of heaven. He finds the very glory of beauty in "the world and night and star-enclustered space". The moon silently walking the night in silver shoes calls forth his most exquisite art. When he narrows his gaze to the minor objects of nature there is still a quality of light about them: Creep and Shellover glimmer like the dew-shine in the rising moon; the wings of rooks are gilt-lustered; the weed by the white stone is twice lovely as light and shadow play across it. There must always be light in beauty because light was the first creation and beauty is God's sign-manual—"it was for joy God made the rose". And as soon as we say this it is obvious that something more enters into de la Mare's idea of beauty than colour and pattern and refracting surfaces. Though indeed the marvel of mere visual beauty, of sight itself, never ceases to move him. Just as to him the words by which poetry is achieved are scarcely less fascinating than the accomplished poem, so he is endlessly intrigued by the miracle of sight, the wonder of the mechanism of the eye, that "strange device which alone divides the seer from the seen".

But there is no escaping the fact that de la Mare's interest in the beauty of earth is seldom pure. It never has the simply sensuous motive of Keats or the youthful Wordsworth. It is more akin to Wordsworth's mature vision; but whereas Wordsworth saw nature as infinitely significant because it conveyed the presence of the divine Being, the principle of all life, to de la Mare nature is a reflection of the ideal beauty which is his life-long pre-occupation. Wordsworth's deduction from experience of natural beauty is religious and satisfying, de la Mare's is aesthetic and disturbing. De la Mare cannot forget that "the loveliest thing earth hath a shadow hath", and falls thence to ponder on "the beauty of heaven's shadowless asphodel"—an expression in which "heaven" and "asphodel" cancel each other out, leaving "shadowless"—implying a deathless perfection—as the significant word. He would unloose the bonds of life and by the thought of immortality make of the changing the unchangeable. Till that far-off event can come to pass he takes consolation in the hints of immortality worldly beauty affords. Even the most familiar aspects of beauty come upon him every time with a shock of strangeness and wonder. Beauty is never to be accepted, understood. A chance-seen face will ravish him, for its loveliness "hovers a mystery between dream and real"; and the beauty of the green-leafed willow is secret as a dream. Natural beauty invites the supernatural: the shady creek has its Naiad, the nook of the wood was sometime visited by a stranger inhumanly lovely. There is always the possibility that the beauty of natural phenomena is more than a reflection—"as if the inmost secret of what they are lay open in what they seem"; and perhaps by gazing on and on in love the harebell may be persuaded to give up its strange secret.

Nature's beauty seems sometimes to clamour for mystic interpretation—as the sea that swung by

> Dazzling dark-blue and verdurous, quiet with snow,
> Empty with loveliness.

And so, as the sound of lapping waves brought to the exiled sailor-man a vision of England, "witchery-sweet", earth's surpassing beauty moves de la Mare to dreams of the ideal beauty of his longing. Deep as he is in love with England's hills and valleys, he is "happy beyond words" when he escapes in dream to where the landscape is England with a difference, its air milky and sweet, its habitations touched with unreality, its creatures elfish and gentle and enchanting. Temporal beauty evokes a lost loveliness he calls Arabia, a place imagined as just beyond the limits of imagination. De la Mare, the Wanderer in quest of the holy vision, is tempted aside by the lure of earth's beauty, but he knows this must fade in ashes so he puts it by and goes on into the night where alone the eternal beauty is to be found. The wandering wind and the dark restless breakers speak to him of an unimaginable beauty. The pilgrim of beauty, he scans mortality for the inhuman ideal which lures him restlessly on.

Beauty

Far have I come and far must fare.
Noon, night and morning prime
I search the long road, bleak and bare,
That fades away in Time.

On the world's brink its wild weeds shake,
And there my own dust, dark with dew,
Burns with a rose that, sleep or wake,
Beacons me—"Follow true!"

No one has less cause than de la Mare to complain,
"Where is beauty? Gone, gone is beauty from me."
He dwells with beauty—and not the beauty that
"must die". He has travelled far and secretly beneath
the distant skies of the moon: he has found there a
paradise—and he brings back a flower, fragrant if
invisible, in proof, and has learned a music he has not
skill to breathe. He indulges a fascinating notion of a
"real" self—of which the mortal self is but a shadow
—already traversing that paradise of dream. It is a
paradise otherwise not easy of access, and the poet
asks why the gods, having dowered man with Fantasy, yet hang veils of fog between him and his infinite dreams. The visionary gets his glimpse—perhaps of a face "with eyes of light unchangeable whose
grave and steadfast scrutiny" pierces through all
earthly memory—and then must go "back into life's
wild banishment", to meditate on a beauty so strange
and frail that human touch would ruin it as a zephyr
breaks the still surface of a pool.

Often he speaks in parables—under the similitude
of Arabia or the Dark Château—of the fairer, flawless
world of his imagination. Beauty is a "strange spirit"

that leads on before him through youth and age and the final night of death. And almost his ultimate word is of a "beauty no mortal life could e'er fulfil", the steadfast loyalty of his soul, a changeless vision that at last shall call the wanderer home.

It is the high privilege of rare and exalted minds thus to worship the ideal of a transcendent beauty. But such worship may grow immoderate and bring with it a penalty in the form of an agonizing "homesickness" and loss of peace. The importunate beauty of a visionary face takes the savour out of life. The remembrance of the far country, glimpsed and lost, becomes "a wasting fire", "a vain and unassuageable desire". Thought is worn down to "the wreckage of a wasting dream", and even love is now "but the memory of what woke once but re-awakens not". Inexorable beauty grows a burden: the brains of those who follow its siren decoy grow travel-wearied and dull with despair. In one mood de la Mare sees in his dream of beauty nothing but perilous pride of the imagination: he recognizes it as a pagan passion, and recommends his soul to surrender it at the feet of God.

This, however, is a solitary instance, and at that only a warning against extremism. De la Mare knows very well that the action of beauty is as beneficent as its absence is fatal. But for the light of beauty the human mind would be "wholly a dark and dismal spot". When he bids the child, "Drink, happy mouth, from Wisdom's well", it is not learning or prudence he is commending; as Wordsworth's Lucy was to be educated by clouds and stars, so de la

Beauty

Mare completes his precept—learn wisdom from
beauty:

> Bid the strange world to sigh thee now
> All beauty hath to tell.

The Traveller shows the spirit refreshed by beauty
as a tired-out child by sleep:

> Thus beauty may
> Pierce through the mists that worldly commerce brings,
> Imagination's blindness wash away,
> And—bird at daybreak—lend the spirit wings.

In *Fare Well*, that lyric of so profound significance,
we are bidden to look always on beauty with the intensity of regard and love which we should give to it
if we were about to lose it for ever, for beauty, like
God, both gives and takes away. Beauty induces in
the heart a sense out of which it can but sigh a *Benedicite* on life, and the poet's prayer of repentance is
that where he has been blind beauty may come to
make atonement.

There is earthly beauty, and there is the ultimate
beauty laid up in heaven. Somewhere between the
two is the beauty of dreams, the dreams of a poet.
Think of the dream-landscape of *The Assignation*,
apparently commonplace, frosty meadow and frozen
brook, but given strange significance by a white
horse, "aged with time and toil, and now at peace",
which grazes and presently raises its gentle head to
show "eyes blue as speedwell, tranquil, morning-fair";
there is a sense of mutual recognition, of something

103

planned in the long-distant past, and the dreamer—
one racked with illness—feels his soul solaced by the
secret symbol. The scenery of dream is a constant
factor in de la Mare's experience, and always of a
quality to keep him in touch with the infinite:

> Stealthy in onset, between wake and sleep,
> Such scenes, more moving than the earth can show,
> May, self-created, in mutation sweep,
> Silent and fugitive as April snow.

But the trance-condition of dream is not a necessary
medium. The poet's mind is perfectly receptive, and
flashes of magical beauty bring their revelation at any
time: in the silence that comes with the planet of
evening's silver flame, with echo that trembles away,
shadows coming and going in the firelight, a face of
fancy in an empty house, a spectral voice that calls
through the dusk, the phantom children who are
always liable to appear. A bird will approach like a
messenger from out there, and with a low sweet call
be gone. And, above all, music—music which dis-
solves the obscuring, distracting colour-screen of the
beauty of this world to reveal the lovelier vision of the
mystic scene, rapt, ecstatic, enchanted, solemn.

The final feeling about de la Mare's poetry of
beauty is that, ineffable as is earth's beauty, the beauty
of earth is not enough. The poet ever looks past it to
the ideal beauty; his ghost "sits at his eyes" and
thirsts for snows even more untroubled; he longs to
explore "in slumber soft" the charms of the unknown
before waking brings him back to everyday. All

Beauty

beauty on earth is darkened by the recollection of a
sweeter, stranger loveliness half-conceived and half-
forgot. Wood and pool, rose and dewdrop keep the
secret of an escaping phantom beauty. Every poem
is a supreme adventure into a world where the question and the knocking on the moonlit door may,
though they never do, bring a response more illuminating than silence. Words of wisdom and courtesy
are whispered in that world of dream, and the dreamer
burns to go back and hear those words again, so that
he might perhaps remember. We cannot sound the
depth of the passion of de la Mare's dream of a beauty
beyond all earth's imagining. How flattered, how
glad then ought we his English readers to be to feel
the sincerity of his tribute to the present and tangible
beauty of *England:*

> No lovelier hills than thine have laid
> My tired thoughts to rest:
> No peace of lovelier valleys made
> Like peace within my breast. . . .

CHAPTER VIII

Love

THERE is much love-poetry in English, and most of it is in the first rank as poetry. As an expression of love, however, it does not often satisfy a reader who takes love seriously—one who holds with Chang Chao that "passion holds up the bottom of the universe, while genius (merely) paints its roof". It is unusual, because it is difficult, for a poet to allow love this fundamental position and function. A poet cannot put love first: to him life comes first, his art next; love may perhaps come third. It is simply impossible to imagine Shakespeare being, for more than an occasional hour, obsessed by love. In consequence, far from unlocking his heart in the *Sonnets*, all he does is to permit us two peeps through the keyhole. With Burns the love which was doubtless for him more centrally placed was a fly-by-night emotion again unacceptable to the true lover for whom the diagnostic of love is permanence. Browning knew love as few poets have done, but most of his love-poetry consists of studies of other people in love. The women-poets, being women—"For love is of man's life a thing apart; 'tis woman's whole existence"—have found it easier to go straight to the mark, and there is no questioning the authenticity of the love poems of Elizabeth Browning and Emily Brontë.

Love

This last observation offers a clue which may be worth following up. The existence of a feminine streak in the nature of a poet may be necessary for the profoundest knowledge, or at least the frankest expression, of love. Such a streak in Matthew Arnold explains the strangely moving quality of the two groups of love poems, *Switzerland* and *Faded Leaves*. The same thing in Hardy makes his love-poems his highest achievements in verse. Your strong masculine natures can be complete masters of the meteoric course of romantic love, but for a sensitive understanding of the love which burns with steady intensity for a life-time and beyond there seems to be needed a touch of that mystery of strength adulterated by weakness which is the crowning glory of a woman's heart. There can be small doubt that de la Mare is privileged to share this condition, and it would be a fair deduction from his non-erotic verse that the love-poetry of such a writer must be supremely excellent. It is in fact this, and more: it is, or some of it—that part which speaks of love and death—so individual and new as to be all but unique.

We may first glance at that small proportion of his love poems which go to an established note.

> After the songless rose of evening—
>   Night. . . .
>   You in the valley standing. . . .
> Beauty hid your naked body,
>   Time dreamed in your bright hair,
> In your eyes the constellations
>   Burned far and fair.

Or,

> Come in thy beauty! 'tis my love,
> Lost in far-wandering desire,
> Hath in the darkling deep above
> Set stars and kindled fire.

This, though beautiful, is or might be romantic love. The magnificent conceptions are introduced with great imaginative power, but astronomical hyperbole is a commonplace in the language of love. There needs some special element, some mixture of the alloy of sadness, to turn the metal of de la Mare's love-poetry into a stuff of marvellous and unknown virtue. At least one would have said so before the perfected art of *The Burning-Glass* gave us *To a Candle*, a study of beauty in sleep in the person of "one I love", and a poem which illustrates a childhood-love harmony peculiar to de la Mare. In the still burning of his candle the poet looks down with deep emotion on such loveliness that fear takes him; but the lashes stir on pure cheeks and the milk-blue blood pulses under the silken skin. Then, with a characteristic thought—

> Time hath spread its nets in vain;
> The child she was is home again—

he breaks through to the spirit beneath the beauty: he feels that the face, so innocent, so wise, was made by love, that the visible form is the dwelling-place of something divine, prisoned there because "it was for joy God shaped the rose". So he comes back to bodily beauty, to the white sweet hand above the gentle breast, and falls into a dream over his candle-shine.

Love

Here too fall *When the Rose is Faded* and *The Shade*,
with their beautifully visualized absence, and the exquisite poignancy of *Not One*, where the lover keeps
his vigil, vainly grieving "That not the briefest
moment—yours or mine—Can ever come again".

As we approach the poems which give lyric form to
the agony of loss through death, we come to a group
voicing the equally vital if less poetic conception of
inseparableness in life. How intimately interwoven
are two lives whose very dreams are mutually involved.
The beloved has been awakened by a dread cry, out
of a dream, of "He is dead!" and the lover, comforting
her fears, asks what could have prompted the dream:
was it the future speaking, or the remorseful crying
of love?—

> Or, haply, was it I who out of dream
> Stole but a little way where shadows course,
> Called back to thee across the eternal stream?

This reads like high romance, but is instead the stark
literalness of love as understood by de la Mare. So
again in the poem called *Life:* the lovers, having come
together, feel experience has now nothing significant
to offer till death—

> We who in one strange kiss
> Have proved a dream the world's realities
> Need heed no more of life.

Yet life, the commonplace, must be lived, and between the moments of ecstasy the lovers must keep

109

the loveliness of love buried cold in their hearts. *Twilight* gives, with such flawless brief perfection that it can and must be quoted in full, a spiritual unity born again of the intense emotion of beauty:

When to the inward darkness of my mind
I bid your face come, not one hue replies
Of that curved cheek, no, nor the faint-tinged rose
Of lips, nor smile between the mouth and eyes:
Only the eyes themselves, past telling, seem
To break in beauty in the twilight there,
And out of solitude your very ghost
Steals through the scarce-seen shadow of your hair.

In all these poems there is a perfection of form which is in itself a symbol and embodiment of love.

We have yet to come to the most remarkable of de la Mare's love poems, but the poems already considered furnish grounds for a claim which I am disposed to make for him as the writer of—I must not say the greatest: greatness is adjudged by time—but of the most beautiful and deeply satisfying love-poetry in English. For love's swift splendours and ironic pain we may go to Shakespeare and Donne, for its pathos and fire to Keats and Burns, for melodious emotion to Shelley and Tennyson; but of love as an infinite tenderness, unfading and undying, the sign and seal of the perfect blending in perfect union of two spirits, I see in de la Mare the supreme master. There is not much of this ideal love in English poetry, but it inspired both the Portuguese Sonnets and R.B.'s response, *By the Fireside*. Nearly all de la Mare's love-poetry has this love for its theme and its heart, and since the theme inspired an unfailing technical excellence of the highest order, de la Mare's love-poetry stands with that part of his work which is most assured of immortality.

I have suggested that among these love poems, all supremely beautiful, there is one group which, in its essence and quality, is almost unique. "From Sappho to Spenser, and from Shelley to Mr. Swinburne"—so runs a never-to-be-forgotten eulogy of the *Sonnets*— "many poets have written excellently of love"; but (if one may venture to substitute a feebler adversative for the triumphantly hyperbolic original) until the coming of Hardy and de la Mare one note was inadequately sounded—the note of loss. This is doubtless as it should be, and I am not complaining. The splendour of love is a present and positive thing, and the poet-lover best serves those who are not poets, and perhaps not even lovers, by singing the infinite delights of happy love. And of course the plangent note of loss is heard from time to time. . . .

O western wind, when wilt thou blow
That the small rain down can rain!
Christ! that my love were in my arms
And I in my bed again.

*　　*　　*

I wish I were where Helen lies;
Night and day on me she cries;
And I am weary of the skies
　　Since my love died for me.

*　　*　　*

111

O Mary! dear departed shade!
Where is thy place of blissful rest?
Seest thou thy lover lowly laid?
Hear'st thou the groans that rend his breast?

        *   *   *

But she is in her grave, and oh!
   The difference to me.

        *   *   *

Come to me in the silence of the night. . . .
   Come back`in tears,
O memory, hope, love of finished years.

        *   *   *

Rose Aylmer, whom these wakeful eyes
   May weep but never see,
A night of memories and of sighs
   I consecrate to thee.

        *   *   *

            . . . beseeching
That still, despite the distance and the dark,
What was, again may be.

        *   *   *

And so all the night-tide I lie down by the side
Of my darling—my darling—my life and my bride,
   In the sepulchre there by the sea,
   In her tomb by the sounding sea.

        *   *   *

Come to me in my dreams, and then
By day I shall be well again,
For then the night will more than pay
The hopeless longing of the day.

        *   *   *

Cold in the earth—and the deep snow piled above thee,
   Far, far removed, cold in the dreary grave!
Have I forgot, my only Love, to love thee,
   Severed at last by Time's all-severing wave?

These are among the classical places of lament, and yet where, except in the first and the last, is there the stark abandonment of love lost in death? It would be unkind to suggest that most of the passages express the luxury of grief rather than its heart-break, but some such reflection is inevitable if one's standard of comparison is the bleak despair of a poem of Hardy— *The Going*, or *The Voice*, or *The Phantom Horsewoman:*

> Queer are the ways of a man I know:
>   He comes and stands
>   In a careworn craze,
>   And looks at the sands
>   And the seaward haze
>   With moveless hands
>   And face and gaze,
>   Then turns to go. . . .
> And what does he see when he gazes so?
>
> They say he sees an instant thing. . . .
> A phantom of his own figuring.
>   . . . everywhere
>   In his brain—day, night—
> Does he carry that vision of heretofore:
>
> A ghost -girl-rider. And though, toil-tried,
>   He withers daily,
>   Time touches her not. . . .

What is it that constitutes the difference?—for difference wide and deep there is. What is the nature of the new tone that so intensifies the poignancy of the expression of loss in love-poetry? I think it is the tone of intimacy, the sense not only of two loves but two lives

sundered—two lives that have not only come together in passion but have grown together through
time and long-enduring love. The earlier poets knew
all there is to know about love as a swift emotion: it
has remained for some later ones to bring to love-
poetry all that is meant by life-long companionship,
and the shattering pain of its termination by death.
Perhaps what Hardy, and de la Mare after him, have
done is to turn from the outer courts of romantic love
to its central shrine, which is domesticity.

Unfortunately, permanence in love somehow
touches the mind less thrillingly than do the ardours
of its first stages, and for a hundred readers who feel
the call of romantic love (that lovely and immortal
kind)—so that love-poetry means for them, "Oh,
Mary, at the window be", or "Good night, good
night, parting is such sweet sorrow"—there may be
one who will not smile derisively at that word
domesticity but recognize its connotation of a yet
lovelier passion that pervades the soul and outlives
time.

Turning then to de la Mare's poetry of the loved
and lost, we find first two prelusive poems in which
some sorrow, strange, bitter, profound, lends to love a
sense of loss as desperate as death itself. There is that
terrible poem, *Be Angry Now No More:*

> Be angry now no more!
> If I have grieved thee—if
> Thy kindness, mine before,
> No hope may now restore:
> Only forgive, forgive! . . .

Love

Ask of the winter rain
June's withered rose again:
Ask grace of the salt sea. . . .

The Tudor sonneteers and lyrists wrote thus of love's
dark disquietudes—

Forget not yet the tried intent
Of such a truth as I have meant:
My great traveil so gladly spent
Forget not yet!

But the Elizabethans rather enjoyed their pain—as
they enjoyed everything else in life—and never wrote
with such broken intensity of feeling as is shown in
this anguished thing of de la Mare's. In *The Tryst* (a)
the sorrow is more subtly suggested. Ostensibly the
lovers are to meet for delight, the wild delight of
sharing an absolute solitude—"There of your beauty
we would joyance make"—but the music is "wistful",
and the poem is drenched in despair. All the lover can
offer is a "perchance"; all he can suppose is that "Two
might happy be"—"*might* there not rest be found";
the climax of his hope is but a "silence wherein to sing
love's requiem"; and even to that the answer is "no".
The compelling rhythmic beauty of the poem, by
reason of which it claims supremacy, is inextricably
bound up with the melancholy of the theme—a com-
munion of sadness, insubstantial but strong, and
exquisite almost as happiness.

Next, a group in which, though death has evidently
played its cruel part, the uttermost extremity of loss
is not yet present. That lovely brevity, *In Vain*, reads,

with its knocking and its stars, like a pale proleptic echo of the bitter grief of *The Ghost* (b). Were it not for its tone of austere despair we should hardly grasp its theme. I am not sure that we do grasp it, but we are well content to be made dubiously sad, and to savour the faint unearthly music of its four perfect stanzas. Just so quietly—even more quietly sad is *Where?* with its exquisite though less haunting form. The third of these three, all of a kind, is *April Moon*,* where pain is robbed of its urgency by being filtered through the deliberate moon-imagery.

To these three poems of the pathos of irremediable separation, and before we come to its tragedy, must be added that strange ambiguous poem, *The Monologue.* The picture is one out of the distant past, of a prisoner who listens for tapping or voice from someone imprisoned in an adjacent cell, and the realism of the

---

* This poem has a special technical interest in its close (though unintended) parallelism with Wordsworth's *She Dwelt Among the Untrodden Ways.* For the material solitude of Wordsworth's first stanza de la Mare presents the abstract isolation of strangeness and rarity; in the second, where Wordsworth brings into comparison the hidden violet and the lonely star, de la Mare's image of unpretentiousness is that of a little moon whose shade is lovelier than its light; in the conclusion, after the fact of death has been stated, Wordsworth says indefinitely, "Oh the difference to me", but de la Mare, carrying on the moon simile (and thereby breaking the simplicity of the prototype form), gives specific consequences of the moon's setting—darkness, solitude and fear. The Lucy poem has an artistic singleness beyond that of *April Moon,* and its opening is more effective, but the more elaborate imagery of de la Mare's second and third stanzas can hold its own with the simpler thought of Wordsworth's. Each poem is highly characteristic of its author, and there is nothing to choose in beauty and sincerity.

descriptive touches—the bird fluttering at the high barred window, the straw in the corner, the rack, the bread and water—is so strong that it is with some difficulty that the reader gets behind the allegory to the lover yearning for communication with the dead, driven to doubt by the unbroken silence, yet feeling that silence is best.

> Nay, answer not.
> Let still mere longing make
> They presence sure to me,
> While in doubt I shake:
> Be but my Faith in thee,
> For sanity's sake.

That last desperate cry warns us that we are already, and at last, within range of the final group of love-poems: those in which we are brought face to face with loss itself, utter and desolate, the ultimate and irrevocable separation by death, and yet in which we hear the tones of a deep and passionate intimacy stretching beyond the mortal barrier. It is the supreme poetic expression of love in desolation, of a companionship made even closer by death, that puts these poems among the greatest of all love-poems, and makes them among even these unique. The theme is one which Hardy, almost at the same time, was enriching with the profound sincerity of his genius; but de la Mare, with no less tragic intensity of feeling, adds a far greater mastery of the poetic medium.

The poems, a mere handful of seven, comprise *Vigil, The Remonstrance,* the two poems called *The*

117

Ghost, and three from *The Burning-Glass—Not Yet,*
Thou Art My Long-lost Peace, and *The Vision.* The
seven poems should be printed together in some
beautiful format, to become the priceless possession
of all lovers, both those strong in happiness and those
broken by affliction. I would place *The Remonstrance*
first in the slender volume, if only because its right
to a place there at all is disputable. Whether life or
death be the setting of the love here told is not
apparent, but the sadness of death is upon the poem,
and the beloved is not, at any rate, altogether of this
earth: she is a "vision grave", she has "ghostly lips
and eyes". The glory of the poem lies in its assertion
of the diagnostic of love, which is complete surrender
of self:

> O vision grave,
> Take all the little all I have!
> Strip me of what in voiceless thought
> Life's kept of life;

lies, too, in the picture of the haunted house of the
poet's life:

> Still 'neath its walls the moonbeam goes
> And trembles on the untended rose;
> Still o'er its broken roof-tree rise
> The starry arches of the skies;
> And 'neath your lightest word shall be
> The thunder of an ebbing sea.

Then there should suddenly flare out the sombre
passion of *Vigil,* with its laconic line, its heart-stirring
rhythm. The lover watches with his book and a dying

fire, while the winds call from the darkness to mock his loneliness. But he is not alone:

> O ghost, draw nearer;
> Let thy shadowy hair
> Blot out the pages
> That we cannot share;
> Be ours the one last leaf
> By Fate left bare!
>
> Let's Finis scrawl,
> And then Life's book put by. . . .

The yearning pain of the poem would be unbearable were it not for the living presence of the ghost-beloved that gives to sorrow an almost equally intolerable beauty.

The Ghost (b) plunges yet deeper, and brings us to the middle of the sequence. It is good to remember that there are other poems to follow, for the lacerating grief of this poem, its stark despair, making the form hard and jagged like ice, is not the note on which this book of love should end. Again the lover waits in loneliness and darkness:

> "Who knocks?" "I who was beautiful
> Beyond all dreams to restore."

With hope-wearied hand he draws the bolts and looks out, to find as so often before only the grey and vacant night—

> Nought but vast Sorrow was there,
> The sweet cheat gone.

The colloquy with this ghostly voice recalls another
with a more satisfying, almost substantial, revenant,
in Browning's poem, *The Householder*. The situation
is the same—"Savage I was sitting in my house, late,
lone"—and this love is as great as the other—

> When in a moment just a knock, call, cry,
> Half a pang and all a rapture there again were we;
> "What, and is it really you again?" quoth I.
> "I again, what else did you expect?" quoth She.

Nor is there any lack of intimacy in the colloquy that
follows, but it is a cheerful intimacy that sounds
almost barbarous after the gaunt sorrow of the other.
The clue to the difference is to be found not in
Browning's "optimism" but in the last line of his
poem—

> "I end with—Love is all and Death is nought!"
> quoth She.

To the poet, now as ever, love is all, but the questioning of the twentieth century has made the separation
of death a more bitter thing than it was when Browning wrote.

We have reached a nadir, where grief can go no
further. Sorrow must be stilled: despair must have an
end. The four poems which close the sequence show
loss no less real, no less dominant and absorbing, the
pivot on which life turns, but assuaged by time and
love, made gracious, fruitful, a source of beauty and
peace. The motif of *The Ghost* (a) is peace, that divine

Love

concomitant of love; the poem is a benediction, full
of peace and dellamarian loveliness, pronounced over
the bowed heads of all sad lovers:

> Peace in thy hands,
> Peace in thine eyes,
> Peace on thy brow;
> Flower of a moment in the eternal hour,
> Peace with me now.

> Not a wave breaks,
> Not a bird calls;
> My heart, like a sea
> Silent after a storm that hath died,
> Sleeps within me.

> All the night's dews,
> All the world's leaves,
> All winter's snow,
> Seem with their quiet to have stilled
> in life's dream
> All sorrowing now.

And yet this condition, infinitely beautiful as it is,
is a negative one, and love is never content with negation. The winning back to happiness is completed in
the poems from *The Burning-Glass*. *Thou Art My Long
Lost Peace* is a more creative version of the last poem:
peace now has a richer and more positive content; it
gives vision and understanding. Beneath the "even-
ing-gilded wave", symbol of peace, there is felt "the
unmeasured deep" of eternal reality. Beyond the
beauty of the waking hour, which "feigns Reality"

and yields a pining of body for body, is the strange longing of the spirit for what has gone from earth's day into "cloaked Eternity". So that if there is woe for earthly loss there is the rapture of spiritual assurance.

Not Yet, almost an epigram, fits into its place as showing sorrow and loss at a stage where they can be handled almost playfully. Few poems, even on this exiguous scale, enjoy such flawless finality.

> "Not love me? Even yet!"—half-dreaming, I
> whispered and said.
> Untarnished, truth-clear eyes; averted, lovely
> head:
> It was thus she had looked and had listened—how often—
> before she was dead.

The sequence closes in a poem which in strictness does not belong to it at all, and yet fitly concludes by lifting the personal into the universal. *The Vision*, a supreme and perfect poem, has for its theme the Eternal Beauty which is the dream and desire of every poet: "past speech or thought", "life's haunting mystery", "life's changeless vision", "changeless and immortal and serene". But eternal beauty is the aching ideal of every lover too, particularly of the lover whom death has made lonely, and it is open to the lover to read into this poem—into its "starry face bound in grave strands of hair", "garnered loveliness of all I see", those hands, those breasts, those eyes— to see here the "steadfast desire" of his own "soul's loyalty", and to feel that he too would wish his last thought to be, "Spent is this wanderer, and you call him home".

*   *   *

In case there should be any who were unable to complete the sentence I began to quote about Shakespeare's Sonnets, and who even more unaccountably failed to recognize that combination of romantic enthusiasm with classical soundness of judgment which uniquely indicates George Saintsbury, let me supply the rest of the rolling period: "From Sappho to Spenser and from Shelley to Mr. Swinburne, many poets have spoken excellently of love; but all that they have said could be cut out of Shakespeare's Sonnets, better said than they have said it, and still leave enough to furnish forth the greatest of poets."* A claim so magnificently made establishes itself without the necessity for proof (even if "proof" were possible in matters of this sort), but in any case it ends specifically with Swinburne, and it does seem to me that the two more recent poets, Hardy and de la Mare, have had something to say of love that cannot be "cut out" of the Sonnets for the

---

* I love these lusty championings of the supreme masters. An equally pleasing one was put forward some years ago by the music critic of *The Times* in connection with the performance of a newly discovered fragment of Beethoven: "It did not, evidently, occur to him (the spokesman of the B.B.C., who had half-apologized for the appearance of the piece in the programme) that one idea which came from Beethoven's brain, even if he abandoned it as not worth pursuing, is likely to be worth more than all the music of the 'composers of secured position to-day' put together."

simple reason that it is not there. If the tragedies must
be explained by something tragic in Shakespeare's
life, it is not a tragedy of love. The affairs of Shakespeare's loves, as far as they are reflected in the
Sonnets, compose not a tragedy but a tragi-comedy;
and for loss itself, its only place in the tale is to give us
such lines as these:

> Then can I drown an eye, unused to flow,
> For precious friends hid in death's dateless night;

> Thus have I had thee, as a dream doth flatter,
> In sleep a king, but waking no such matter;

> Love's not Time's fool, though rosy lips and cheeks
> Within his bending sickle's compass come;

lines made poignant not by grief but by their extreme
beauty.

This by the way. There is no question of competition with Shakespeare, nor does de la Mare's love
poetry depend on the note of loss which gives it its
peculiar quality. It is a true, passionate, and intensely
lovely contribution to the lover's anthology. That a
contribution of this sort should come from a poet
whose interests are in the main confined to the spirit
world will not surprise those who know that love
belongs to that world too.

(I append a list of the poems of this chapter in the
order in which they are mentioned.)

Love

THE LOVE POEMS OF WALTER DE LA MARE

The Unchanging
The Invocation
To a Candle
When the Rose is Faded
The Shade
Not One
The Death Dream
Life
Twilight
Be Angry Now No more
The Tryst (a)
In Vain
Where?
April Moon
The Monologue

The seven
{
The Remonstrance
Vigil
The Ghost (b)
The Ghost (a)
Thou Art My Long Lost Peace
Not Yet
The Vision
}

CHAPTER IX

Childhood

FEW poets betray less aspiration to the title "poet of man" than de la Mare. He stands at the opposite pole from Chaucer, Wordsworth, Browning. Even Shelley's airiest fancies are bottomed in a profound philanthropy. But de la Mare is not, poetically, interested in mankind.* How should he be? He seeks a world "less unsatisfactory" than this, and it is man that constitutes the plainly unsatisfactory element in the world. Man at his best—a More, a Goethe, a Dorothy Wordsworth, a de la Mare—goes far to justify the proud claim that he is little lower than the angels. But it was Wordsworth himself who, having declared "the dignity of individual man", inquired,

> Why is this glorious creature to be found
> One only in ten thousand?

Is it any wonder if de la Mare, his soul aching for perfection, turns his back on the appalling mess that "man has made of man", turns to contemplate the supreme loveliness of the world of spirit?

There are critics of narrow vision who call this escapism, and de la Mare has bowed to their sordid reproof to the extent of a few poems of pity for human

* The word "poetically" needs stressing, because humanly, as well as in his prose stories, de la Mare is tirelessly interested in everyone and everything.

126

suffering—*Poor Miss 7, In the Dock, Drugged, Hospital, On the Esplanade, The Slum Child* (though there goes more than pity to this), *Of a Son*, and a few others. I cannot feel that we ought to ask for more in this sort. Pity is well within the compass of all good men: we go to de la Mare for something rarer. In the broad sense mankind is not his "proper study". But there are two conditions under which man is ideally interesting and beautiful: when he is a child, and when he is in love. Of love and childhood de la Mare has much to say.

There is, of course, poetry *for* children, and there is poetry *about* children. Of de la Mare as a writer of poetry for children I have said something, and shall not say much more, except that he seems to me to enjoy an unchallengeable supremacy in this kind, if we take, as the two criteria of excellence, first, aptness to children's taste, and second, high poetic quality. There are nine-and-twenty ways of writing verse for children: one of the best is the frolicsome doggerel of the nursery rhymes, but this art has been lost with other simplicities—when we try to recapture it we are as likely as not to arrive at something "ruthless", like the rhymes of Harry Graham. Lear and Lewis Carroll revel in their own cleverness and wit, and achieve poetry for children by a fortunate accident; Blake sees the child through his own mystic absorption, Words-worth studies him with almost painful seriousness, Stevenson observes him humorously; A. A. Milne and Eleanor Farjeon join in the children's games, guiding and suggesting like a jolly elder brother or a charming teacher; Allingham and Rose Fyleman write out of sheer delight in children's fancies, Longfellow and Jean Ingelow out of a tender parental love, Swinburne out of a sensuous joy in the exquisiteness of a child's body. All these ways are "right", and what each way has produced for the delectation of young and old is beyond praise. But there is yet another way, and it is de la Mare's. He alone has written as an inspired child: rather perhaps as if the genius of an inspired poet should take possession of the personality of a delightful child. With all a great man's matured wealth of experience, he has been able to keep the priceless gift of a child's feeling for life.

Apart from an occasional hint of "the wisdom I lost as a child" (*In a Library*) there is no question of endowing children with any of those powers of insight which Wordsworth apostrophized in the Immortality Ode, so bringing upon himself the blandly devastating criticism of Coleridge. What de la Mare does is to keep, side by side with his man's sense of power, the child's sense of humility. O Man! he exclaims—thy dreams, thy passions, hopes, desires! —all but the riddles and fancies of a child's fond universe. More than this, to "keep innocency" is the sovereign antidote for the mortal disease of cynicism. Life is full of terrors, but the child hears only a fine music, and the man who can keep the illusion through life keeps his head high and his soul unsullied.

> O if with such simplicity
> Himself take arms and suffer war,
> With beams his targe shall gilded be,
> Though in the thickening gloom be far
> The steadfast light of any star.

Childhood

And even though sooner or later life trample him down, he shall fall unconquered, because he has kept unto his "last content" the pure bright vision of a world that evil cannot make ugly.

> Quenchless shall burn in secrecy
> The flame Death knows his victors by.

Parents of young children have been known to deny to de la Mare an understanding of the child mind on the ground that he allows the thief at Robin's Castle to carry away Robin's two beauteous little children in his bag along with the rest of the plunder. They see a similar obtuseness in Stevenson, who wrote a poem for children about all the wicked shadows going tramp, tramp, tramp with the black night overhead. But if these poems are read in the spirit in which they were written, with the glowing and enchanted unreality of the one, the arch humour of the other, no child of normal sensitiveness gets anything but joy out of them.* That de la Mare comprehends a child's night-fears, and sympathizes with them (but without morbidity) is shown in the poem *Hark!*—"My little Charles is afraid of the dark". He demonstrates over and over again that he has done what many parents and educators of the young fail to do—has got inside

* There is only one harmfully frightening poem in the whole de la Mare range—*The Little Creature*. With the hammering insistence of its refrain, "My great-grandam—She was a Witch!" and its multiplied hints of evil, it seems to me to be a poem not to be read to children (though the one certain thing about children is that their ways are not our ways—and the poem is, after all, only a serious version of *Little Orphan Annie*.)

129

The Poetry of Reality

the child-mind, seen with the eyes of a child, felt with its feelings, thought its childish thoughts. We have already seen Ann "getting together" with the ghost-child in *The Phantom* (a), and little Louisa peeping at Death in *The Keys of the Morning*. Surely we catch a glimpse of the soul of a child in *The Buckle:*

> I had a secret laughter,
>   I laughed it near a wall:
> Only the ivy and the wind
>   May tell of it at all—

and another in *The Window:*

> Behind the blinds I sit and watch
> The people passing—passing by,
> And not a single one can see
>   My tiny watching eye. . . .
> They do not even know I'm here,
>   Nor'll guess when I am gone.

So too, the dark joy that accompanies the child's discovery of the secrecy of thought is hinted in the reflection that Mrs. Earth and Mrs. Sun can do many things,

> But all that I'm thinking of, ever shall think,
>   Why, neither knows.

The poem called *The Bells* shows poet and ploughman held by the music of the bells with whose sound the church tower trembles, while the ploughman's three children

130

Childhood

In the green grass placidly
Played undistracted on, as if
What music earthly bells might give
Could only faintly stir their dream.

The Sleeper has been mentioned for its touch of the
supernatural, but it is no less admirable as a study of
childhood. It is a special but not uncommon type of
little girl that is so perfectly pictured in the opening
lines:

As Ann came in one summer's day
    She felt that she must creep,
So silent was the clear cool house—

and the conclusion shows an equal understanding:

And as Ann peeped, a cloudlike dread
    Stole over her, and then
On stealthy, mouselike feet she trod
    And tiptoed out again.

The complex of the child's feelings—nameless, in-
apprehensible for the most part, but perhaps with a
nucleus of fear lest she should make her mother cross
by waking her—is hinted with much exactness in
that "cloudlike dread".

Sometimes it is a rarer kind of child whose roving
and constructive imagination is portrayed with equal
insight. Such were the children who listened to the
stories Martha told them in the hazel glen; such is
the boy through whose understanding eyes we see
Nicholas Nye. Or the child—a girl this time, I think
—who feels that someone is always sitting there, in

K

the little green orchard; who, at twilight, has heard
voices calling softly in the little green orchard.

> Not that I am afraid of being there,
> In the little green orchard;
> Why, when the moon's been bright,
> Shedding her lonesome light,
> And moths like ghosties come,
> And the horned snail leaves home:
> I've sat there, whispering and listening there,
> In the little green orchard.

The question will always arise whether poetry
written for or about children is likely to be enjoyed,
or even ought to be enjoyed, by children. With
writers like Stevenson, Blake, Swinburne and de la
Mare the question may be answered by asking
another—do adults enjoy the poetry which these
writers wrote for adults? The answer to that question
is that some do and some do not, and the answer to
the other question is that those children enjoy the
child-poetry who are like the adults who enjoy the
adult-poetry. None of these poets writes for the
ordinary man or the ordinary child. They write what
they must write, and have not condescended. Their
child-poetry, like the rest of their poetry, is written in
the language of poetry, which is a foreign language.
Mr. A. A. Milne leaps to the mind as a writer with a
different aim. He tells little stories in metre; and the
dainty metres are handled with such ease that the
child does not know that what he is hearing is "poetry" at all—as of course it is not. He thinks he is
hearing—as indeed he is—an amusing story told in
sentences that are strangely charming, alluringly

pretty and dancing; but he has not to rise above himself to any understanding of "poetry". De la Mare always makes this demand, and in *Peacock Pie* the demand is heightened as the book proceeds. The first section, *Up and Down*, consists chiefly of simple poems for children but many are touched with beauty, and at any moment imagination may be invoked, as in *The Huntsmen* who rode their horses up to bed, and *The Horseman* that opens the book:

> I heard a horseman
> Ride over the hill;
> The moon shone clear,
> The night was still;
> His helm was silver,
> And pale was he;
> And the horse he rode
> Was of ivory.

Twice, in *Old Shellover* and *Miss T.*, the poet passes far over the heads of his little readers, to the lasting joy of his larger ones. Nothing, at first blush, could seem more innocent, childish, than the duologue between Shellover and Creep. Yet do but think of that night-enchanted garden, bejewelled with dew and gazed upon by the rising moon; given over to the lowliest forms of life, snail and slug and old Sallie Worm; the higher beings, alien and tyrannous, man and thrush, withdrawn to distant lands of sleep, so that all is stillness and shimmering beauty, broken only by the tenuous drawl of the wakeful molluscs: do but project yourself in spirit into that brilliant dream-like scene, and you will know by direct experience what the primitive creation was like. This,

133

through the magic of a rhythmic lift, is wonder and poetry. So inspiration deepens, through such miracles as *The Thief at Robin's Castle*, *Nicholas Nye*, *The Pigs and the Charcoal Burner*, *The Changeling*, *Silver*, to that last section, out of the reach of any child, to be achieved by long devotion to beauty, to poetry, to life—the section of the marvellous songs, ending with the *Mad Prince* and *The Song of Finis*. Setting aside these two great poems, what happy children are those who shall find among their rhymes such starry stanzas as these to set them dreaming:

> Twilight came; silence came;
> The planet of Evening's silver flame;
> By darkening paths I wandered through
> Thickets trembling with drops of dew.

> But the music is lost and the words are gone
> Of the song I sang as I sat alone;
> Ages and ages have fallen on me—
> On the wood and the pool and the elder tree.

But who shall chronicle or adequately praise all the verses de la Mare has written to give delight to children: the swift enchanting tales, the poems about animals and birds, fairies and fancies? No less delightful, and of more permanent value as throwing a more penetrating light on life—a search-light as against a Chinese lantern—are the poems written for adults about children. These are on the whole the work of later years, just as the best of the other kind are to be found in the earlier books. They range from an amused interest in the child's reactions to life's predicament—Tom and his wonder at the long narrow box the men have brought to Miss Emily's house opposite, Pollie and her lovable vacuities, the little girl who was changed by a passing military show from tearful pity for a dead hare to a flushed desire to "go and see it skinned", Jack who was tired of books and longed for the meadows and the sea-shore—from this amused observation they range on through a more serious interest to a tender and sometimes passionate love.

He subjects *The Slum Child* to a scrutiny as close as that he gives to *The Snowdrop*, and pierces through the "evil, filth and poverty" to "a self beyond surmise". Similarly he searches the child-like face of *A Young Girl*, but though he hears her thoughts singing he knows that her dreams and her inward innocence are close-shut from his understanding. He studies the tiny features of *A Child Asleep*, and, as a master of the art of expression, envies the epigrammatic power of its creator. He enters into the bewilderment of the "questioning mite" who finds her love for animals discredited by hard-headed elders. He wonders what it was that Velasquez talked about to the "solemn plain-faced child" while he painted her portrait, but thinks he understands her well enough to engage her in an "abstruse small colloquy". As he cries out at the tragedy of *The Blind Boy* who is unaware of the lovely things that light reveals "on this all-marvellous earth", he notices a smile that betokens perhaps some "exquisite whisper of sound". He admires the serene aloofness of the boy reading by the stream in whom a transcendent rainbow calls forth but a smile and a memory. He goes into all the gorgeous details of

Jack's multitudinous reading, and appraises his love of the music and meaning of words.

Some of his interest is given to recollection of himself as a child—how, "in passionate innocence", he bought a present for the grown-up *Lucy*, whose "once-loved face" now "comes back, my dear, among the distant dead"; how he found "a respite, a solacing, deep as the sea" in the peaceful Sundays of long ago; how (a remote, vivid, precious memory, this), as the early sunlight stole over the pictures in his bedroom "in those eternal hours I spent with myself as a child", his heart overflowed with tears at the thought

> that love unsought, unspoken, unshared, unbetokened,
> Had mastered me through and through,

and yet was kept a secret even from the loved one.

The foregoing paragraph is an understatement of a vitally important fact which received some notice in a previous chapter. De la Mare's interest in "himself as a child" is intense, because he feels that childhood is the period of life in which the mind is fresh, sensitive and responsive to contacts with the world of spiritual reality in a degree impossible to adult life. There is a lovely expression of this conception in *The Traveller*, where the poet tells how "sleep brings comfort to a tired-out child"—

> Sleep to a body so pure and exquisite
> Like manna it is, at gilding sunrise seen;
> The senses so untrammelled that as yet
> No more than frailest barrier lies between
> Soul and reality.

136

Childhood

The idea inspires some of the short stories, is elaborated in *Early One Morning*, and is continually present in the poetry. My recollection of my own childhood and observation of other children convinces me that de la Mare's account of childhood is true only for a minority of children, perhaps only a small minority. I am tempted to call these children unfortunate, because when their childhood is past they are compelled to spend the rest of their lives regretting the spiritual intimacies which passed with it. But they are also deeply blessed, in that the "celestial light" of their "angel infancy" permanently enriches the visionary faculty, and one cannot doubt that de la Mare's imaginative dream is the flower of his childhood experience.

Though all the poetry that de la Mare has written for and about children is instinct with love, yet—until quite late—an explicit love for children seldom receives direct expression. It is heard (of course!) in that classically beautifully apostrophe, *The Birthnight: to F.* It is seen in the intensity of the picture drawn in *Winter Dusk*, one of those still, rapt interiors so characteristic of de la Mare: the mother reading to her two children—a third child, a spirit, hovering near—the mother intent on her story:

> Yet when, the story done, she smiled
> From face to face, serene and clear,
> A love, half dread, sprang up, as she
> Leaned close and drew them near.

It is seen in two of those marvellous epitaphs round

137

which that lovely book, *Ding Dong Bell*, is written: in
the one that begins,

> Here lyeth our infant, Alice Rodd;
> She were so small,
> Scarce aught at all,
> But a mere breath of Sweetness sent from God;

and especially in the tenderness of the "little odd
stone" the benighted lovers found almost hidden in
brambles:

> Be very quiet now:
> A child's asleep
> In this small cradle,
> In this shadow deep.

And surely it lies at the heart of that "brief song", so
strange and lovely and pathetic, of "the world's little
children magic hath stolen away".

But love grows more personal, more tender, in
later poems. What exquisite pain is in *Sallie's
Musical Box:*

> Once it made music, tiny, frail, and sweet—
> Bead-note of bird where earth and elf-land meet.
> Now its thin tinkling stirs no more, since she
> Whose toy it was, has gone; and taken the key.

What deep yearning in the "Heaven bless you
child!"—one hears de la Mare's own voice—of *And
so to Bed*. The charming humour of *Safety First*—

> Do not mention this young child's beauty as he stands
>   there gravely before you;
> Whisper it not, lest there listeners be. Beware
>   the evil eye!—

does not conceal the love that inspires it—for the
"innocent marvel", the "beauty and promise"—or
the "labyrinth" of thought and praise and gratitude.
And in two poems love comes from the profound
depths of passion. In *The Sleeper* (b) the poet stands
looking down on the girl who lies so still, as still as
death—

> Yet her young cheek with life's faint dye
> Was mantled o'er; her gentle breast
> Like sea at peace with starry sky
> Moved with a heart at rest.

And he knows, he is deeply moved to think, that at the
call of a bird or a beam of day she will awake to the
miraculous bread and wine of life. Again, in *The
Glance* he tells how—

> Dearest one, daughter! at glance of your brow-
>   shaded eye
> Fixed gravely in all its young scrutiny dark on
>   my own—

his soul was lifted to a vision of the world's creation,
with the solemn angelic music and the dream of love
in Eden; but, the child knowing nought of this, he,
with bowed head, "could but clasp your cold hand in
my own, and was dumb as the dead". A lovely experience incident to fatherhood, but requiring the
poet for its interpretation.

Indeed, it is useful to remember that in these later
days de la Mare is both father and grandfather. Bio-
graphical information is often a hindrance to the

understanding of a poet's work, but some of de la Mare's child-poetry is brilliantly illuminated by a glimpse of his love for his own children and grandchildren. Not that we are *necessarily* to see portrait-miniatures in the Sallies and the Pollies and the Anns, the Lucys and the Jacks and "my little Charles"; in the lovely ones, the lorn ones, the dear ones; the small child who suffered such a quick change of heart over the dead hare, the boy who with mild and serious eye dreams of war as chivalry and pomp and music, or the other one whose twilight reverie must not be disturbed by the bringing of candles; the little child who talked to himself as he ran along, and the little boy who stood watching Rachel at the piano; the children who shared with the Fairy on the topmost bough a loving secret under the Christmas tree, the young boy whose beauty and promise stirred fear in the hearts of those who loved him. We have already seen that in one or two instances the father stands confessed: about these others there is always the charming possibility. But the tenderness with which every child in all the poems —even poor Henry!—is touched shows up strongly in the light of the deep and beautiful personal feeling in which it originates.

Children are the flowers of the human garden.

> Child, do you love the flower
> Shining with colour and dew
> Lighting its transient hour?
> So I love you.

But more goes to it than that. There is a special

rapprochement between de la Mare and the child-mind. There is in him a "lost child" who has never ceased to regard life as something to play with—and is prepared to justify the attitude before High Heaven (*A Dull Boy*). Assessing (in his seventh decade) the brighter and more obscure elements in his vision, he calls them "Two gardens for two children—in one mind". The general opinion is with St. Paul, that there comes a time when it is good to "put away childish things", to assume a protective coat of worldly wisdom and cynicism; but I have said enough to show that I believe close contact with the ultimate life of spirit is only to be preserved by those who, like de la Mare, can keep, with the matured mind of an adult, the simple heart of a child. That Shakespeare kept the magic combination is shown, I think, by his turning from the great tragedies to the romantic comedies, to the creation of Imogen, Perdita, Miranda, Ariel.

The tenderness of de la Mare's feeling for children, his nostalgic recollections of childhood days, and his sense that virtue goes out of life as the years pass are blended and triple-distilled in that miracle of loveliness called *Dreams* (a)—

> Be gentle, O hands of a child;
> Be true: like a shadowy sea
> In the starry darkness of night
> Are your eyes to me.

> But words are shallow, and soon
> Dreams fade that the heart once knew;
> And youth fades out in the mind,
> In the dark eyes too.

The Poetry of Reality

What can a tired heart say,
Which the wise of the world have made dumb?
Save to the lonely heart of a child,
    "Return again, come!"

CHAPTER X

Humour

I F one were illogical enough to attempt to base a distinction between poetry and prose on difference of content, one might find specious support for one's argument in the suggestion that the antithesis of poetry is humour. Science, history, philosophy may be given poetic form, but not humour, not this:

> "But in a tragedy", I insisted, "the catastrophe *must* be led up to, step by step. My dear Brown, the end of the hero *must* be logical and rational."
> "I don't see that", he said, as we crossed Piccadilly Circus. "In actual life it isn't so. What is there to prevent a motor-omnibus from knocking me over and killing me at this moment?"
> At that moment, by what has always seemed to me the strangest of coincidences, and just the sort of thing that playwrights ought to avoid, a motor-omnibus knocked Brown over and killed him.

How fearfully would the razor-edge of that fine thing be blunted in anything but stark prose. Consider, too, the relation, that of an inverse ratio, which apparently exists between the greatness of a poet and his equipment in humour. Shakespeare breaks all rules, but four of the claimants to second place among English poets, Spenser, Milton, Wordsworth and Shelley, can all be shown, from their writings, to have been totally devoid of a sense of humour.

143

Not that I want to press this relation, or agree with Mr. Charles Morgan that a sense of humour is a vice—sapping faith, darkening spiritual truth, the enemy of singleness of mind, and necessarily absent from the make-up of really great men: "Jesus had no 'sense of humour'. Shakespeare had none." That the all-round mind of Shakespeare included a sense of humour is as plain as that life is a humorist: for proof —his retirement to Stratford at fifty; it is the people who take themselves and their work seriously who sit tight to seventy or more and long to "die in harness". The man, again, had a pretty sense of humour who could lavish his life-blood on an intellectual Hamlet and then let him be utterly taken down and bested by an illiterate digger of graves. That Jesus did not lack humour is shown in the gospels more than once. How else are we to explain His advice to His disciples to take the lowest seats at a feast so as to get kudos out of being invited to move up higher? or His kindly testing of the woman of Canaan with His (if not humorous then heartless) question, "Is it meet to take the children's food and cast it to dogs?" with His instant response to her ready acceptance of the cue? Doesn't His neat evasion of the trap set for Him by those who asked if it was lawful to pay tribute to Caesar bear witness to the same gift? When Jesus stood up from writing on the ground, to find the crowd of accusers silently melted away, didn't He have to suppress a smile as He turned to forgive the sins of the woman taken in adultery?

The four humourless poets instanced were freaks. So, on the other side, was that other very great man (and greatest of letter-writers) Charles Lamb, whose singleness of mind took the form of humour. For most men—and Mr. Morgan is right to this extent—it is true to say that if the sense of humour bulks too large in them they never get anywhere. But a complete absence of humour leads to a premature hardening of the mental arteries, and to that blind and godless thing, uncharity. Would Mr. Morgan's Ferrers have been a smaller man if, recognizing the Admiralty's difficulty, and denying Christ for Christ's sake, he had been able to say, "Error? Well, perhaps! Who knows?" and so got on with the job, instead of forcing Karen and the First Lord to supply his deficient sense of humour and make the little concession between them?

As for poetry and humour, some sort of opposition between them seems to have been always accepted. Up to our own day (the modification is to be noted) humour and poetry have been as oil and water: it has been recognized that they will not mix, and they have been kept apart. Without going further into the definition of poetry, we may say that it is generally taken to connote imaginative vision and that transmuting quality not otherwise to be described than as poetic fire or passion; and it appears at all events that poetry in this sense has in the past not admitted of humour. There has been a definite division of poetry into serious and humorous, and humorous verse, abundant and glorious as it is in our literature, has always worn the less exalted crown. Revel as we may in the splendid laughableness of Hood, of Barham and Praed, of Calverley and Lear and Lewis Carroll, or in the comic side of Chaucer, of Dryden and Pope, of Goldsmith and Burns, we know that their excellences, or the excellences of their humorous verse, are not poetic in the sense defined. Poetry has been different from prose in this, that its humorous side has been kept for the shallower levels of life. The poetry that we feel to be most significant is entirely serious. Life, the poets seem to say, is, after all, real, life is earnest. And they feel that to interrupt the serious expression of beauty and truth with a quip would be sacrilege.*

Thus far the older poets. But we have changed all that. To us their position seems paradoxical: we feel no inherent incompatibility between poetry and humour. The twentieth century finds humour as necessary as fresh air, and places it a close third to beauty and truth: indeed, Walter Raleigh threw out the intriguing suggestion that "humour may become for us what beauty was to the Hellenic world". The highest poetry no longer rejects humour as an element. There is a clear hint of this development in Shakespeare, and Bottom, with his ass's head, sleeping grotesquely in the lap of the exquisite Titania, foreshadows the union of humour and poetry that had to wait three centuries for its consummation.

At present, perhaps, the change has not gone very far. The bulk of verse remains, as yet, either definitely serious or just funny; but in a limited number of cases there appears an entirely new blending of poetry and humour which may prove to be the gift to literature of

* Some of Shakespeare's puns and the conceits of the metaphysical poets may be held to show that this rule is not quite universal.

146

the early twentieth century, as romanticism was that of the late eighteenth. The phenomenon makes its appearance in various forms. One of the earliest instances is to be seen in Hardy's little poem called *An August Midnight*, where a cosmic conception and a moment big with eternity are associated with "a long-legs, a moth, and a dumbledore", and an inimitably described "sleepy fly, that rubs its hands". This is a new thing, that a great poet should, even as his soul reaches out into immensity, keep hold on the funny side of life.

A similar juxta-position, in lighter wise, may be observed in Newbolt's poem, *The Faun*. Roaming by the brook-side, the poet espies the genius of the pool, with ears a-prick, shaggy flank, and little pair of hooves; but

> Under his satyric grace
> Something manlike I could trace,
> And the eyes that mocked me there
> Like a gleam of memory were. . . .

In the poem the joy of earth and a very tender father-love are wrought up into intense and singing verse, but through all there runs the sly jest of the unfolding of the identity of the faun, the "little goat", which can break audaciously in the flagrant pun—

> Sternly I replied again,
> "You may spare your boasting vain;
> All that you can do, I did
> When I was myself a kid. . . ."—

without shattering the charm, so beautifully har-
monized are poetry and humour.

The change can be measured in one direction if we
place side by side with certain characteristic lines
from Wordsworth—

> That we can feed this mind of ours
> In a wise passiveness,

or,

> One impulse from a verbal wood
> May teach us more of man. . . .

W. H. Davies's voicing of the same instinct:

> What is this life if, full of care,
> We have no time to stand and stare?

To the modern poet creative idleness is as essential as
ever, but he does not take it so seriously: he does not
go out to be wisely passive, but to stand and stare
"like sheep and cows".

The new mode is so immediately attractive, and
suits so well the irresponsible spirit of the age, that it
has less difficulty in creating its own public than some
other infringements of tradition have had. But both
the classically educated and the half-cultured reader
are troubled, for instance, by *Grantchester*. It is an admirable example of the humour-beauty synthesis.
An English landscape poem, with the tranquil
dreaming beauty of *The Gardener's Daughter*, is
scattered freely with expletives and scraps of German,
which are absorbed as easily as shouting children in a

148

forest. The inferior topographical section being omitted, as it readily may, there is no faltering in the diction, the vision, the lift and swing of poetic passion, and yet the beauty of the first half culminates, with perfect propriety, in that "spectral dance" of

> A hundred vicars down the lawn;
> Curates, long dust, will come and go
> On lissom, clerical, printless toe;
> And oft between the boughs is seen
> The sly shade of a Rural Dean. . . .

while the music and the intense feeling of the last section reach what only a superficial mind feels to be an anticlimax in

> oh! yet
> Stands the Church clock at ten to three?
> And is there honey still for tea?

One might go on to show how well this bizarre mingling of opposites suits both the temperament and the manner of the more recent moderns.*

The theory of the matter was given us by Yeats in *The Cap and Bells* a few years before the practice began. The jester, finding the young queen cold to the message of his soul and his heart, offers his last gift:

> "I have cap and bells," he pondered,
> "I will send them to her and die;"
> And when the morning whitened
> He left them where she went by.

* e.g. T. S. Eliot, *Sweeney Among the Nightingales*, Robert Frost, *The Telephone*, the animal poems of D. H. Lawrence.

149

She laid them upon her bosom
Under a cloud of her hair,
And her red lips sang them a love song,
Till stars grew out of the air.

The Fool has always been a sentimental fellow, but
for the high purposes of love he has hitherto felt compelled to lay aside his folly. Even Lamb is quite touch-
ingly serious in his letter proposing marriage to
Fanny Kelly; it is only in the letter answering her
rejection that he becomes again his prankish self. But
Yeats suggests that love and humour may unite on
equal terms, and succeeding decades have effected the
fusion of humour with other forms of beauty.

De la Mare's part in the story is full of interest. He
is, of course, not one of the great humorists, but his
laughter-sense is strongly developed, and is a genuine
factor in his fantasy. His contribution to the new
species is considerable (much larger, for instance,
than that of Chesterton, who, excellent poet and
mighty humorist though he was, preferred, in his
poetry, to be either one or the other, and to be both
together only in prose). This is something of a consequence of de la Mare's preoccupation with children,
animals and fairies, for there is no more instant
embodiment of the beauty-humour combination than
a child, an animal, or a fairy. It is this combination,
together with the lovely verse-form, that gives *The
Thief at Robin's Castle* its unending fascination. Out of
the spell of the story, all complete with its miniature
pity and terror, there rise moments of delicious
humour that assuage the tension and actually enhance

the unashamed beauty of the telling. So the poems *Nicholas Nye* and *Old Shellover* throw over the lowly creatures that are their theme a veil of beauty through which their comic aspect is seen shining unobscured. What a smilingly beautiful picture is called up by the line which forms the refrain of *Maerchen*—"The Cat looked long and softly at the King". With fairies the problem was an easier one, and the beauty and humour of *Grim*, for example, is perhaps only the regulation mixture found in all (prose) fairy tales. Poems like *Sooeep* and *The Scarecrow* (a) and (b) and *The Pigs and the Charcoalburner* are the fruit of a different faculty, that of perceiving the beauty of things which to the common eye are merely grotesque. Who else could have followed the three stanzas about the big Pig and the little pigs, and the greedy sound of their grisling and their gruzzling as they chuffled for truffles and mast, with the marvellous concluding stanza of Night walking her starry ways while the Charcoalburner broods over his sullen fire? With de la Mare it is the natural climax of the poem; with any other poet (certainly any earlier poet) it would have been a sort of inverted anti-climax, a too sudden change from the ridiculous to the sublime.

How inseparable are the strands of dreaming beauty and humorous realism in *The Englishman*. The sailor's grammatical errors are caught up in the same music that expresses his vision of England.

> "Ay, ay, I could not be mistook;
> I knew them leafy trees;
> I knew that land so witchery sweet,
> And that old noise of seas."

151

The Poetry of Reality

Tennyson, in a similar emergency (say, *The Sailor Boy*), gives us beauty only, Wordsworth (*The Sailor's Mother*) no beauty at all. Think of Sam's memories of how, as a boy, he used to lean from his window in the moon to watch the tumbling billows: those memories are altogether lovely, but they do not omit his father's snores, or to tell how once he saw a mermaid, and heard her

> Calling me, "Sam!"—quietlike—"Sam!"
> But me. . . . I never went,
> Making believe I kind of thought
> 'Twas someone else she meant.

And there is no less humour, and at least what may be found of beauty in middle-aged romance, in Sam's final reflection:

> P'raps, if 'twere *now* my son,
> P'raps, if I heard a voice say, "Sam!"
> Morning would find me gone.

A delightful picture of a clear green gloom, with fairies spinning, a white tree-maid in a rain-sweet glade, throstles and a stamping bunny and Old Wat chin-deep in bracken, is framed in the shouts of a straddling boy called Longlegs. *The Song of the Mad Prince* itself starts from "Who said Peacock Pie?" And the sublime imagery of *The Tryst* (a) includes, among the many strange and beautiful rendezvous appointed by the lovers, one, a hole hollowed by Noah's mouse beneath the chair of slumbering Omni-

152

potence, and another, "in Time's smallest clock's minutest beat".

In the same way humorous narrative poems rise easily into moments of sheer loveliness. That jolly tale, *Off the Ground*, never loses touch with beauty. But the best example is *Sam's Three Wishes*, most of which is in the tune of the opening—

> "I'm thinking and thinking," said old Sam Shore,
> "'Twere somebody *knocking* I heard at the door";

but which once on a page turns to this.

> Yet Spring came again with its green and blue,
> And presently Summer's wild roses too,
> Pinks, Sweet William, and sops-in-wine,
> Blackberry, lavender, eglantine.
> And when these had blossomed and gone their way,
> 'Twas apples and daisies and Michaelmas Day—
> Yes, spider-webs, dew, and haws in the May,
> And seraphs singing in Michaelmas Day.

Take again those little memorial verses that spring up from the delicious prose of *Ding, Dong, Bell* like daffodils on a lawn. All have a melancholy beauty perfectly fitted to the occasion, and some have a delicately pointed humour that sounds no note of discord. In one the beauty will predominate:

> Three sisters rest beneath
> This cypress shade,
> Sprightly Rebecca, Anne,
> And Adelaide.
> Gentle their hearts to all
> On earth, save Man;

The Poetry of Reality

In Him, they said, all Grief,
    All Woe began.
Spinsters they lived, and spinsters
    Here are laid;
Sprightly Rebecca, Anne,
    And Adelaide.

In another it is present only in a touch of blunt
sincerity:

    Here lies my wife,
    Susannah Prout;
    She was a shrew
    I don't misdoubt:
    Yet all I have
    I'd give, could she
    But for one hour
    Come back to me.

In the lines on Fanny Meadows, who died of a consumption, poor lass, in May 1762, the tender pathos does not prevent life being presented as a bright and breathless game, with Death for "he"—and

    'Twas "One, two, three,
    And—out goes she".

And in three of them the blending lies in the rendering of complete reverence with epigrammatic brevity.

    Poor Sam Lover,
    Now turf do cover;
    His Wildness over.

The word "wildness" expresses an attribute that de la

Mare loves: you have it again in the matchless simplicity of—

J.T.

Here's Jane Taylor,
Sweet Jane Taylor,
Dark,
Wild,
Dear Jane Taylor.

And briefest of all—

Here lies old bones:
Sam Gilpin once.

The evolution of this new species, the poetry of beauty-humour, seems to me to be a fact of much significance. It has been intolerable that two such divine things should have been kept apart, that a poet has felt compelled to descend from Pegasus, abrogate his function, change his tune, whenever laughter has tickled his soul. (Imaginative prose has found the gulf less hard to bridge: witness Browne and Carlyle. But even here we have made the identification more deliberate and complete, in *The Napoleon of Notting Hill*, *The Crock of Gold*, *The Happy Hypocrite*, and *The Three Mulla-Mulgars*.) What the new poets have learnt is how to remain poets while indulging their humour, how to express the humorous view of life in a form having all the beauty and moving force of poetry. And it gives me enormous satisfaction to be able to show de la Mare playing so important a part in the only unquestionable advance that poetry has made since Wordsworth.

Thus beatified, humour becomes a true facet of the

155

dellamarian genius. Humour in the ordinary sense of the word (the humour of Falstaff, *Pickwick*, and *Three Men in a Boat*) is among the most delectable fruits of the human mind, but it has little to do with the mystic dream. It is a necessary help to the understanding of life, but only of the rough and tumble of the world of appearance. I am with Mr. Morgan to that extent: for an approach to the essential life of the spirit we need something more than the assemblage of somewhat brutal and entirely human impulses which constitutes a "sense of humour". But beauty-humour is another story. It is a factor, I think a newly-developed factor, in divine life and vision. If there is laughter in heaven it will not be that kind of laughter which Hobbes defined as "a passion of sudden glory" but a passion of delight in some surprising display of beauty and love.

We come down to earth, if to a thoroughly enjoyable corner of earth, when we take up the book in which de la Mare enters into competition with the professional humorists. *Stuff and Nonsense* is amazingly good, and full of that noble English humour, nonsense for nonsense' sake. Moreover, one may find, embedded in the golden amber of laughter, not a few flies of pure fantasy. A poem that might have come straight out of *Peacock Pie* is that one in which the poet says he feels dizzy at "the mere idea, per se", of a year's happenings being packed into a day:

> In four and twenty hours to see
> Like phantoms in a dream flit by
> Between the smiling earth and sky
> A whole year's birds, flowers, seasons fair.

Humour

There is something richly quaint, with an unmistakable flavour of mystery and magic and beauty, about the Vhatka that is heard deceptively ahking in the sky at night, and has to be hunted candle in hand like the Snark. There is a subtle intellectuality about the problem of relativity as posed by Little Jane and the Fisherman. The old dislike of the butcher's trade is still here, supplemented by a shuddering antipathy towards the ironmonger with his ghastly stock of sinks and pails. And de la Mare the animal-lover is seen in *March Hares*, *Witchcraft*, the Finis mouse, and particularly in *Quack Hunting*. Ducks are the supreme example in the bird-world of the beauty-humour synthesis, and as such have inspired more than one poet, notably F. W. Harvey, whose verses on the subject have claim to be classed in the "new species"

> From troubles of the world
> I turn to ducks.
> Beautiful comical things. . . .

De la Mare's poem might be put there too: it is unbrokenly beautiful and tender, and most charmingly funny.

> When evening's darkening azure
>   Stains the water crystal clear,
> It's a marvellous sweet pleasure
>   A small coracle to steer
> To where in reeds and rushes
>   Squeak and chuckle, sup and suck,
> A multitudinous company
>   Of Duck. . . .

157

The Poetry of Reality

And while the dears are feeding, with
Their tails behind their backs,
I make my nightly score—I count
Their quacks.

There is the altogether delicious story of the small hermaphrodite who lived beside the silver Brent but went off to Peru because he couldn't stand the other imps, from Surrey and Kent, calling him Master Middlesex: a tripping, dainty poem full of playful humour and with more than a hint of beauty.

For the rest, the fun is of the irresponsible knock-about sort, hugely enjoyable.* I like Judge Jessop, who persuaded a Bisop (with the h out) to convince his neighbour that the hyssop on his wall was house-leek. It is pure fooling, but carried through with a flawlessness worthy of a better cause. For the Bisop-hyssop rhyme—Miss Sitwell doesn't trouble to take the h out, but rhymes bishop and hyssop as they stand: I don't know which of the two expedients should be regarded as the more licentious. De la Mare's honest if brutal way of solving the difficulty is adopted for the purpose of achieving other recalcitrant rhymes:

She would ride in her gig
In nine fronts and three wig;

* The description hardly applies to the two groups of poems, mildly funny with the unsophisticated humour of Lear, based upon the fallacious theory that "a limerick's best when it's double". The "doubling" certainly gives scope for twice as much nonsense, and de la Mare has taken trouble to get some really funny nonsense in: there is none of the pointlessness which is often the only discoverable quality in a Lear limerick. But the limerick form, single or double, is not native to de la Mare.

Humour

Then descended, like cold suet, to his cabin, and sat
in the dusk on his bunk,
And (if the English language here admitted of it) he
thunk and thunk and *thunk*.

Pleasant enough is Doctor Cox's way with foxes, and
not less so the fun that is poked at the Lady Godiva
Godolphin and her rooted dislike of the "nood". Her
approval of the adequate and irremovable covering
of the lower animals—"sheep are clad in their wool-
lies"—contrasts with Mr. Belloc's objection to the
same principle:

Oh I thank my God for this at the least,
I was born in the West and not in the East,
And he made me a human instead of a beast
Whose hide is covered with hair.

There is likewise a good story of Captain Stingo and
how he saved his ship by throwing his passenger to
the mermaids, told in a rollicking ballad metre, the
old fourteener half-disguised under its lavishing of
extra short syllables.

It is de la Mare taking a day off. His fairy music
has turned into something like that of Calverley or
Gilbert. Sometimes, as in the lovely and admirably
sustained burlesque, *Quickels*, differentiation is provided by gorgeousness of diction. Sometimes there is
an added delicacy of movement, as in *The Waif*:

He lived on acorns, dewdrops, cowslips, bilberries and snow,
A small shy, happy, tuneful thing, and innocent of woe;

159

The Poetry of Reality

or in *The Tank*, which contains the confessions of a clergyman whose name, the Reverend Philip Fish, brought him dreams of the deep—

> I wallow with the whale, or in profundities obscure
> Disport with shapes no waking eye for terror could endure.
> At times I am an octopus, at times I am a sprat—
> And there is a lot of ocean for a little fish like that.

The rollicking fun and lolloping lines of *The Spectre* are brilliantly maintained, and the beautiful story of the Parson of Eard is beautifully told in *Witchcraft*.

There is a judicious admixture of satire—here on the excessive reverendness of Bishops, there on science in general and philosophy and psychology in particular, and on poet-worship (on "seeing Shelley plain") in the dry, epigrammatic verse—very unusual with de la Mare—of *The Bards*, which I cannot forbear to quote:

> My aged friend, Miss Wilkinson,
>   Whose mother was a Lambe,
> Saw Wordsworth once, and Coleridge too,
>   One morning in her p'ram.
>
> Birdlike the bards stooped over her—
>   Like fledgling in a nest;
> And Wordsworth said, "Thou harmless babe!"
>   And Coleridge was impressed.
>
> The pretty thing gazed up and smiled,
>   And softly murmured, "Coo!"
> William was then aged sixty-four
>   And Samuel sixty-two.

160

In *The Burning-Glass*, and in a poem or so from other late books, we find a third kind of humour, neither fantastic nor frivolous—just a quiet smile, out of "the years that bring the philosophic mind", upon human affairs. Chiefly they show a lovely tolerance— of the brainless child (*Pollie*), of the waywardness of women (*Cupid Kept In*), of one's own weaknesses, hardest of all to laugh at (*A Portrait*). Admirable is *Comfort*, the cat's conception of progress—how the ages have brought about that man and puss can share solitude and security within four walls side by side over a warm fire, man in his sheep's wool coat, "me in my fur-about". Some others—*A Dull Boy, Safety First* (both of these probably belong to the new species)—have been mentioned. And there is a dry, salty humour—very successful with children, though they hardly recognize the flavour as that of humour— in the immensely clever poems of *This Year, Next Year*.

In some ways the most complete exemplifications of de la Mare's humorous gifts are to be found in two prose works, *The Three Mulla-mulgars* (or *Royal Monkeys*) and the play, *Crossings*. Both uphold the beauty-humour synthesis with great success; and *Crossings* is pivoted on the humorous and beautiful truth that "human beings of any age who are not happy cannot be wise". Which is a very good note to close this chapter on.

PART II
THE POETRY OF TRUTH

M

CHAPTER I

Truth and the Modern Poet

IF one comments fretfully on the vagaries of contemporary youth, some elderly sentimentalist in
the company is sure to query, "But *are* young
people different from what they always were? Why,
when *I* was a girl. . . ." So with music—it is insisted
that Beethoven too was regarded as a catastrophe in
sound. I don't think such apologies are often ex-
tended to cover modern poetry (or modern painting).
Coleridge summed up the practice of the ages (including the century which followed him) when he
declared that the immediate object of a poem is not
truth but pleasure. Now "modern poetry" is essentially the poetry of thought, of ideas, of truth; with,
instead of form, the pointed word, instead of vision,
the dazzling epigram.

The poet of to-day—the poet of the last twenty-
five years—must face the prose of existence, the utili-
ties of life, the sine-qua-nons. Poetry must be difficult.
Its subject matter must be contemporary: com-
munism, sex, progress, Freudianism, the decay of
civilization; otherwise it is to be labelled "escapist".
Its motive force is not inspiration but the uncon-
scious—a more undisciplined muse.*

The outcome of the new poetics has been a poetry

* The substance of this paragraph is digested from Mr. Louis
Macneice's essay, *Subject in Modern Poetry* (Essays and Studies,
Vol. XXII, 1936). But signs that a counter-revolution is on the way
have not been wanting during the last ten years.

The Poetry of Truth

of violent originality, often illuminating and always interesting—with the varied and continuous interest, the tang and humour, the pungent idiom, of life. It is capable of giving a highly individual impression of beauty, but the pleasure motive has been dropped, and on the whole the new poetry is a vehicle of thought. To this end rhythmic form ("dope") has been abandoned in favour of precise (though not always plain) statement—a prose statement suitable for the transmission of truth, which is now the poet's aim. The poets who were young with the century have, as Arnold* demanded, a "message". They have seen the light, and they are desperately anxious to hand it on. The world is not to be tickled or drugged, but to be saved, and it is to be saved, as ever, by the truth.

The search for truth is endless and enthralling, and there is nothing more important for us as members of the human society than that it should succeed. There can be no right action, except of a temporary kind, that is not based on right belief. That is why most people behave with such persistent stupidity. Their wishes are vaguely for the good, but they have no truth to light them. "The majority of people", it has been said, "are utterly indifferent to truth. . . . Some people never speak a word of truth, or think a true thought, or see anything as it truly is, from childhood to old age." Like the inhabitants of Arber's *Flatland* they live in a world of two dimensions. They touch life in one direction with their will and desire, in

* Thinking of Wordsworth, his own poetry being as pure of "message" as Keats's.

166

another by their senses and feelings. Their minds are flat and thin, unsubstantial as a shadow: drop in an idea and it goes right through, leaving no impression whatever. But truth is three-dimensional. It is solid, permanent, capacious, supporting. To will and sense is added thought, and the result—if the will be good, the senses fine, and the thought strong—is a noble structure that will carry the world. It is to this edifice of truth that the poets, since the end of the first World War (the ranks of the younger poets being strengthened for this purpose by the accession of such elder ones as Yeats, Binyon and—occasionally—de la Mare), have been bringing their planks and girders of conviction—their passionate thoughts on peace and war, liberty and civilization, pain, time and love, age and youth, reason and beauty, death and life. Just as the poets have always done—but with a difference.

Let me give examples, in pairs, of two modes of poetry.

The early Yeats:

> (a) Who dreams that beauty passes like a dream?

and the later Yeats:

> (b) He knows death to the bone:
> Man hath created death.

The early Yeats again:

> (a) When you are old, and grey, and full of sleep,
> And nodding by the fire—take down this book,
> And slowly read, and dream of the soft look
> Your eyes had once, and of their shadows deep;

and again the later:

(b) Here at life's end
Neither loose imagination
Nor the mill of the mind
Consuming its rag and bone
Can make the truth known.

Arnold on the River of Time:

(a) And the width of the waters, the hush
Of the grey expanse where he floats,
Freshening its current and spotted with foam
As it draws to the Ocean, may strike
Peace to the soul of the man on its breast:
    As the pale waste widens around him—
As the banks fade dimmer away—
As the stars come out, and the night-wind
Brings up the stream
Murmurs and scents of the infinite Sea;

and Mr. George Barker on the passing moment:

(b) With burning fervour
I am forever
Turning in my hand
The crystal, this moment

Whose spatial glitter
Travelling erratically
Forward

Touches with permanent
Disturbance the pavements
The faked walls the crevices
Of futurity.

168

Truth and the Modern Poet

Shakespeare on life's illusion:

(a)   We are such stuff
As dreams are made on, and our little life
Is rounded with a sleep;

and Mr. Louis Macneice:

(b) For all the religions are alien
That allege that life is a fiction,
And when we agree in denial
The cock crows in the morning.

Now, whether you prefer the (a) or the (b) items in these pairs, it is obvious that (a) and (b) speak with different voices. More than that, the two voices have different origins—they come from different places, one far and one near. Shakespeare and Arnold and the early Yeats speak from another world than the three-dimensional world of truth. Poetic imagination has lifted them into the four-dimensional world of reality, the world of spirit, the four-dimensional world of which truth is a three-dimensional cross-section and most of life a meaningless caricature. Being ourselves creatures of three dimensions, and conditioned to a three-dimensional world, we cannot conceive the nature of the four-dimensional world of spirit. But in lyric poetry that world is, however incompletely, entered and explored. When the mathematician asked what *La Belle Dame Sans Merci* "proved", it should have been pointed out to him that it proved the existence of a world in which truth is a superficies and mathematics a folly. The world into which we are transported by poetic imagination operating through poetic form is ultimately more important than the immediate human life. But for man to achieve it, and indeed for the poet to imagine it, it is necessary that they shall first make some sort of success of what Wordsworth called

> the very world which is the world
> Of all of us, the place in which, in the end,
> We find our happiness or not at all.

Only by knowledge of the truth can we live in the world rightly and make our guess at its meaning. So the poets join the philosophers in the endless adventure of the quest for truth.

Up to 1945 it was possible to say that with de la Mare, as with Yeats, his "early" poetry was on the whole poetry of reality and his "later" poetry mainly poetry of truth. Nearly all the poetry in the volumes, as published, from *Songs of Childhood* to *Motley* belongs to the former kind, while of the volumes, *The Veil*, *The Fleeting* and *Memory*, less than a score of poems can be thus classified. But any such arrangement is upset, first by de la Mare's preference (like Wordsworth's) for a reasoned rather than a chronological order, shown in the latest collected edition (and by his statement that some of the poems published "later" were written "earlier"); and even more positively by the appearance, in 1945, of *The Burning-Glass*, in which a large proportion of the poems betray, by their form and the effect of that form on the

170

reader, the touch of eternity, the nature of something less tangible than truth and more indestructible.

I shall try, in the subsequent discussion (as I have tried in the foregoing chapters—not always with success) to refer not to volumes but to poems. In most of his poems de la Mare uses the imaginative function, in a lesser number the intellectual—or perhaps it would be more accurate to describe the two functions as mystical-imaginative and intellectual-imaginative. It is those poems which seem to proceed from the second of these two functions that will provide the matter of this second section.

CHAPTER II

Truth and de la Mare

WHAT are the affirmations of the poetry we have been considering in Part I? Here are some of them:

Is there anybody there? said the Traveller.

> Where sleeps she now. . . .
> Life's troubled bubble broken?

> Look thy last on all things lovely
> Every hour.

> What lovely things
> Thy hand hath made!

> God knows
> It was for joy he shaped the rose.

The loveliest thing earth hath a shadow hath,
A hint of death.

> Perchance upon its darkening air
> The unseen ghosts of children fare.

> Peace in thy hands.

> Sweet is the music of Arabia.

> All the enchanted realm of dream
> That burgeons out of night.

172

Truth and de la Mare

Somewhere there Nothing is.

Life's changeless vision that fades not away.

These are not the solid bricks of which the house of truth is built. They are more like those subtle threads that little spiders spin in the spring time, and float off on them into the unknown. But though of gossamer, they are strong as the gossamer chain that bound Fenrir the Wolf; if we dare to trust ourselves to them, they will carry us at least into that O *altitudino* of wonder into which Sir Thomas Browne loved to pursue his reason—to find there what we may find. Whatever we find, all we can bring back is a sense of the strangeness that lies at the heart of Reality, a possession precious beyond all knowledge, but of no immediate use to anyone.

Truth is of a different order from this. It is as useful as light. Truth is the working philosophy of the age. It is the outcome of the deepest thought of the wisest men to date. What is the contribution of Walter de la Mare, a poet, and therefore one of the wisest of men, towards the structure of truth?

The poetry we are to consider was written for the greater part between two wars, in the most depressing period of modern history. The sickening slaughter and monstrous futility of the first German War broke, or at least bruised dreadfully, de la Mare's spirit, and induced a mood of pessimism new to him; more intense than Arnold's, less savage than Hardy's, larger-hearted than Housman's. It had appeared earlier as a recurrent note of lyrical sadness, but now

173

became explicit. Man is presented as a pathetic figure, meeting life with a sigh, troubled by the past and afraid of the future. "Clay-cold humanity" is too poor a soil for the divine tree of life, and God would do well not to turn His hour-glass again. Life has its burdens and its wounds—the bitterest those inflicted by friends. Thought is futile, weaving idle arguments which are as repugnant as they are incredible. Out of this despondent view of man's earthly lot arises a personal melancholy which prompts some beautiful poetry. *The Old Angler*, whether as picture or story, whether taken literally or as allegory, is marvellous, done with imagination and artistic power, bringing suspense and magic, beauty and terror: an idyll steeped in the pain of waste and regret. *The Familiar*, full of haunting echoes of beauty, leads to the confession.

> Peace not on earth have I found,
> Yet to earth am resigned.

In *Music* (b) imagery and feeling rise irresistibly to the climax of the goddess revealed, but the secrets called forth by the throbbing strings are "helpless"; old griefs are awakened, the votaries of love summoned forth are pale-cheeked, and the goddess herself appears snake-haired. In the earlier poem with this title, music dissolved actuality; the actuality now restored is tragic: memories of love are evoked, but they are painful memories.

Elsewhere we find melancholy rooted in a certain fear of life, almost a distaste for life. This again is not altogether a "late" mood. There has always been that longing for the untroubled snows of the far mountains of the mind, and now in poems written under the stress of the First World War and the futile years that followed there is perceptible a bitter weariness leading sometimes to frayed nerves and consequent violence of expression, as in the desperate outlook of *Home:*

> Rest, rest—there is no rest,
> Until the quiet grave
> Comes with its narrow arch
> The heart to save
> From life's long cankering rust,
> From torpor, cold and still—
> The loveless, saddened dust,
> The jaded will.

But presently the feeling becomes more general, finding varied objectives. The self, withdrawing into what should be the rapture and peace of sleep, learns that "in the forests of the mind lurk beasts" which terrorize like ravening packs of death. Looking back on life the poet sees it as a book, strange and fascinating, yet full of horror and folly, meet to be laid aside as a "thumbed thing". His mind, busily idle with the placid transactions of life, finds even the cooing of a dove "dark with disquietude"; and even as he paints the beauty of an old summer-house and the charm of its environment he turns away, "for beauty with sorrow is a burden hard to be borne". Nevertheless the sense of dissatisfaction is nowhere persistent and pervading, as it is with Hardy and Housman, and even before *The Burning-Glass* it had largely succeeded in tranquillizing itself.

In fact, what is more important to note is the constructive conception of happiness. This is put most plainly in the poem *Self to Self*. How to be happy, the poet asks. Not, certainly, by applying the rules of logic to an imperfect world. But take your stand on the wonder of the universe, and thence observe that happiness is in yourself. Life, like the Kingdom of God, is within you. The universe lies in your own eye, to be seen as good or bad. And if you see it as bad you are not alive but dead, for happiness is the foundation of life. Happiness springs from love: it is exquisitely defined as "loving delight"; and without happiness, so defined, life rots at the root. Fully lived, life can be a noble prelude to death, a password to immortality. When the end comes, let it be said that you made the best of the outer world and the inner self. To have been happy in this life is to have won the freedom of the next. A poem from *The Burning-Glass* provides us almost with a formula. Taking the wise, the true, the brave, the gentle for our guidance, we are to create beauty by love and exult in its radiance because "The little we make of our all is our earthly Heaven".

This vital and fruitful philosophy finds implicit expression in several other poems. In *The Slum Child* the poet, while voicing profound sympathy for the misery and degradation of the child's outward life, yet offers awed recognition of the mystery of mysteries, the "self beyond surmise" which, secretly blossoming, provides a well-spring of peace. *A Prayer* calls down a special blessing on those who, in spite of sorrow, fail not from being "the happy, the beautiful, the good, the wise". And *Here Sleeps* presents just such a one:

> A woman true and pretty,
> Who was herself in everything—
> Tender and grave and witty.
> Her lightest turn of foot, hand, head
> Was way of wind with water . . .
> . . . a dear and loving soul.

Love is the talisman, happiness the treasure. Did not old Burton declare love a sudden and sufficient cure for the mental state which he so cunningly anatomized?

An element of melancholy which need not militate against happiness is pity, and the later poetry of de la Mare is rich in pity. His sympathies, like Shelley's, are wounded by the thought of the wronged and suffering ones of earth—the poor creatures driven to suicide, the mis-shapen criminal in the dock, the horror-haunted drug-addict. He brings courage and cheer to the inmates of a hospital; he feels even for the wrecked hull of a once proud ship and the "roofless and eyeless" state of an abandoned church. Other poems show pity inspired with deeper vision. In *The Slum Child*, as we have seen, the poet goes beyond sorrow to show the secret soul riding triumphant over the need for pity. *A Ballad of Christmas*, a great poem with the genuine ballad feeling, floods the heart not only with pity but with mercy and forgiveness. Pity's roots are laid bare in poems like *Shadow*,

177

Public Gallery, and *Of a Son*, where the impression is of man's helplessness at the hands of an incomprehensible fate which descends on this man and passes over the next. In *Dry August Burned*, *Reserved*, and *At Ease* we get an unaccustomed note of anger, at callousness, militarism, and cold hearts unmoved by the call of humanity. *The Widow* is another supreme poem, where grief (as in *The White Doe of Rylstone*) has transcended loss and achieved tranquillity, so that

> far from the world's light she may
> See clearer what has passed away;
> And only little children know
> Through what dark half-closed gates her smile may go.

It is not often that one can say of a poem by de la Mare that it supports this religion or that philosophy. The spirit of the early volumes is Greek in its joy and wonder: if there is mysticism it is not Christian mysticism: the Te Deum of *The Scribe* stands out as exceptional. Yet the world of de la Mare's poetry is continuously, unmistakably and emphatically a spirit world, and it is with something of a sense of shock that we now come upon hints of a tentative materialism. The pathos of that very beautiful poem, *The Corner Stone*, rests on the assumption that the fallen and lichen-crusted granite will remain after man and "life" have vanished.

> Towards what eventual dream
> Sleeps its cold on?

This is not necessarily materialism. The dream of God

doubtless stretches beyond the duration of *homo sapiens;* and the words of the poem do not imply that matter will outlast mind. Nevertheless the poet does seem to be asking the scientist's question; and in *Futility* he is more stickily caught in the trap of the physicist. The "strange heart" of man (or perhaps the questing mind of the poet) is bidden pine no more since

> All this—thy world—an end shall make;
> Planet to sun return again;
> The universe, from sleep to wake,
> In a last peace remain.

This plainly suggests the desert of inanition to which pure science sees creation running down, and though the last stanza calls it but an "idle argument" this is but a refusal of the comfort that the argument was hoped to provide. "Nothingness" was always a deep desire with de la Mare, but it was an individual thing, a dreamless sleep of the spirit, lovely to contemplate if unadventurous: now it involves the terrifying prospect of a lifeless world.

He broods curiously, and with great lyric beauty, over man's place in creation. Entranced by an exquisite scene the poet cannot forbear to pose a "small riddle":

> If hither came no man at all
> Through this grey-green, sea-haunted lane,
> Would it mere blackened nought remain?
> Strives it this beauty and life to express
> Only in human consciousness?*

* A dellamarian paraphrase of the celebrated limerick beginning, "There was a young man who said God. . . ."

This is doubtless idealism rather than materialism, yet again it indicates a certain dubiousness on the nature of reality, and the answer that follows—" idly breaks he in to an Eden"—makes man irrelevant. Another answer is perhaps to be found in the chaffinch and the butterfly of the poem: for them too, in their degree, the scene exists to express its beauty and life; they were the next upward stage, as man is the next again and God the last. Similar doubts as to man's part in creation are seen in *The Flower*. Set against the vastness of the universe is man, transient and lonely. Transient he has ever been in de la Mare, but it was a lyrical transience, a curve in the rhythm of life, not one that left him

> Sighing o'er a universe transcending thought,
> Afflicted by vague bodings of the past,
> Driven towards a future unforeseen, unsought.

We have observed some slight concessions to scientific theories, but in the main de la Mare regards these as frivolous.* The ways of science are not, for him, the way to truth, much less to reality. He gives "an anatomy of his thoughts" on knowledge in *Dreams* (b). He loathes the psycho-analyst's interpretations of the strange and perilous adventures of the dark, just as he distrusts theories of evolution—declaring that "we know apes father no Michelangelo". He is aware that cell and tissue share man's destiny and influence his passions and thought, yet

* It is amusing and instructive to know that though a D.Litt. several times over de la Mare firmly refuses to be admitted D.Sc.

believes that man, the living spirit, is ultimately master. The brain is a marvellous organ, but no one knows its relation to mental processes, and highest thought comes often with an effortless inexplicable suddenness, not by conscious cerebration, while imaginative creation (like dream-imagery) emanates from somewhere other than actuality. Knowledge of the phenomenal world is false unless it be confirmed by feeling and instinct, and the reality which the "timeless self" must come to know is something entirely spiritual, the living fount of love.

One of the truths established in the course of *The Traveller* is that right feeling comes from right thinking, that is, from imaginative understanding. The crisis of the poem occurs when the pilgrim awakes to a recognition of "mind supreme" in the earth over which he is journeying—an allegory of man's discovery of the spiritual nature of the universe. The new knowledge effects a change in his outlook on life, shown in the differing natures of the two visions, one before and one after illumination. The first is the pessimist's dream of man debased and destroyed, of man's evil ways breeding a poison in his blood that shall bring about his extinction. The later corrective vision is that of the triumphant failures, the cravers for something out of reach, following impassioned love to a goal beyond the grave.

There is in all this a certain anxiety of seriousness which represents a falling-off, to one side, from the heights of pagan joyousness. Oddly enough, a divagation to the other side is to be seen in other poems, where consolation seems to be sought in orthodox religion. Man, left alone with himself, is "haunted" by innumerable disturbing questions, and since the imaginative world could no longer provide answers to these questions or to the fears and scruples previously enunciated, a solution is found in Christian dogma. *News*, a strange but successful poem, impressionist and half Eliotesque, notes among the causes of our discontents "An empty Cross on a Hill" —though the conclusion the poem arrives at, "Love is dead", is more universal. *The Snowdrop* is interesting not only in itself but as providing a criterion of religious progress over three-quarters of a century. Tennyson plucked a little flower out of the crannied wall, held it, root and all, in his hand, and murmured, "But *if* I could understand what you are . . . I should know what God and man is". And left it at that. He assumed God, but gave up the effort to understand Him. De la Mare (incidentally, without destroying the flower—an advance in itself) asks the same question:

> I will see what this snowdrop *is* ;
> So shall I put much argument by,
> And solve a lifetime's mysteries.

To find an answer he tries to project his mind into the life of the snowdrop—

> called my soul
> To don that frail solemnity,
> Its inmost self my goal.

The attempt is partially successful:

In this collusion I divined
Some consciousness we shared.

Strange roads—while suns, a myriad, set—
Had led us through infinity;
And where they crossed, there then had met
Not two of us, but three.

He has found God by a mystical process, and understands Him to the extent that both man and flower share in His nature. Much more uncompromising is *The Imagination's Pride*, where man, frightened by his own fancies, is bidden turn for comfort to a Heavenly Father.

Humble thy trembling knees. . . .
His deepest wisdom harbours in thy side,
In thine own bosom hides His utmost love.

These two diverse tendencies seem to be reconciled in the "problem" poem, *The Strange Spirit*.

Age shall not daunt me, nor sorrow for youth that
is gone,
If thou lead on before me.

Who or what is the "thou"? It is not Newman's "Thou"; it changes throughout the poem, appearing now as this, now as that, hovering on wings invisible, menacing the earth-bound spirit, ranging earth, sea and sky—

Bodiless, lovely, snare and delight of the soul,
Fantasy's beacon, of thought the uttermost goal.

In the last line of the poem it is named—"Life of life": one supposes the dellamarian version of the

183

"Life Force", a union of love, beauty and death, with an aspect of deity.

Nowhere is the change of focus, from reality to truth, from intuition to thought, more clearly noticeable than in respect of imagination. The poetry of reality exists in virtue of imagination: imagination is its world, its medium, its end and its cause. Imagination is unquestioned, because there is none to question it: poet and reader are part of it. But now it is held up for examination, its validity is suspect. A bound is set to life, a notice-board inscribed "Sane-secure" is affixed, and the horizons beyond are "forbidden". Man is advised to turn from his search for the immortal rose, the invisible blossom, and take refuge in the wisdom and love of God. However, this is not the last word. *The Decoy* shows the poet, at least, going passionately on with that same endless quest, and *The Catechism* allows imagination, the soul of the poet —not "proud" but humble, yet assured—to assert its place and function: that function is stated with crystal clarity—*not* to tell "truth of the life that is", *not* to bring forth the fruits of faith and hope and a sign from heaven, but to offer "nought wiser than worn out songs of moon and of rose", to have faith in sweetness, to tranquillize frightened eyes with dreams. Thus the argument is brought to an impeccable conclusion. Yet argument there has been, and one remembers a melodious rebuke from *Motley*—

> Leave this vain questioning. Is not sweet the rose?
> Sings not the wild bird ere to rest he goes?
> Hath not in miracle brave June returned?
> Burns not its beauty as of old it burned?—

where the echo of the Sonnets carries its own significance.

If, for a time, the imaginative faculty is given a rest, as it were, the materials of imagination are constantly at hand: the miracle of life and the mystery of death; the mystery of the hidden self, and of a young girl's innocence; the miracle of the earth at dawn, of genius, of the inner eye's sudden brightness; the mystery of the snail's life, and of the snowdrop's being; the mystery of dreams, and of the child's vision; the mystery of night, and the magic of memory. All these elements of wonder are faithfully presented, while the poet's mind plays over them, reflectively rather than imaginatively.

Other poems take us a further step towards that restoration which was completed in *The Burning-Glass* —restoration of the intuitional intimacy with that over-world of which our passing life is a shadow. The air of an October day is full of "omens, monitions, hints of fate", so that the ghostlike sound of a cockled leaf suddenly shed from a sycamore bough is a whisper—"What! And still happy? Thou?" In the dreariness of protracted illness nothing can solace like a dream, nothing seem so significant—though it be but a dream of a starved upland grazed by a white horse. At another time the poet, drowsing over a book of biology, slips into a dream of Eden, and finds it sweeter than any knowledge of genes and chromosomes. A minstrel of unheard melodies lures children and the tired feet of earth-bound wanderers. Silence casts again its spell—"all sounds to silence come". Once more a doubt is expressed as to whether it is

185

wise to venture "out of bounds", to "covet what eye cannot see or earthly longing know"; as to whether the lovely things of earth would be lovelier in an unearthly setting. And the reply is given with succinct finality in *Night:*

> That shining moon, watched by that one faint star:
> Sure now I am, beyond the fear of change,
> The lovely in life is the familiar,
> And only the lovelier for continuing strange.

No man to whom the familiar is ever lovely, ever strange, is in danger of losing touch with the underlying world of unfamiliar reality of which loveliness and strangeness are tokens, or of losing the instinct to wander "out of bounds". Again, in the poem called *Romance* you have the very creed of illusion, which is the poet's creed of reality. The lovely changing lights upon the sea can be referred to their origin in the laws of physics, but to the poet they are delight and desire, love and romance; man likewise is but bone and senses, but there is a seraph in his mind that can praise and soar into the unknown; and the seraph and the praise and the romance of the unknown are more "real" than the physics and the anatomy.

Beauty is imagination realized, brought within the scope of human feeling. Love is beauty in action. Beauty and love operate mainly in the visionary world, but outside it de la Mare has wise things to say of both. He has compiled a nobly abundant anthology called *Love*, in the Introduction to which we may find such significant judgments as these: "The chief value of our earthly life rests on what and on how much we love in it"; "Without love any acme not only of happiness but of understanding is unattainable"; "Love . . . life's transcendent blessing". Among the poems, *News* shows the bitterness of a world where love of God and love of man are dead; and the comment follows in *I Sit Alone*, though here it is not so much a world gone awry that calls for lament as the flaws in life itself. Even these can be healed by love:

> Only love can redeem
> This truth, that delight,
> Bring morning to blossom again
> Out of plague-ridden night;
> Restore to the lost the found,
> To the blinded, sight.

(How terribly true that is—and how nonsensical it must seem to a world where life would sometimes appear to be motived largely by hate and covetousness.) As we have seen, the question is argued out explicitly in *Self to Self*, and a solvent for life's tragedy is again found in love. Loveliness no longer suffices: the poet seeks the profounder condition of happiness, and enforces the imperishable truth that the way to happiness, to life itself, lies through love.

> Loving delight forgot
> Life's very roots must rot.

The philosophic, almost religious importance attached to love and happiness gives these poems high imaginative rank.

It is to be observed that the love to which such importance is attached is the love of St. Paul's *Epistle* rather than that of *Romeo and Juliet*, a wide-spread passion of kindness rather than a passionate feeling for a single person. De la Mare goes so far (in the Introduction just mentioned) as to suggest that "an ardent affection even for an inanimate object . . . is of the same kind as even the deepest devotion to a fellow creature. . . . Liking is to love . . . only a question of degree"—a heresy which cannot live in the company of those passionate poems of lost love that we have already considered.

And finally, death, that endlessly provocative stimulus to man's imagination. De la Mare has ever been pre-occupied with death. As far back as *The Listeners* man is shown "haunted" by his mortality, an "inward presence" which, "unmoved, remote", slumbers not, and "frets out each secret from his breast", and the conception had already appeared in that beautifully patterned crystallization of thought, *Shadow*. Strange that even here, so early, the word "haunting" has crept in:

> A dark and livelong hint of death
> Haunting it ever. . . .

Life, it seems, is death in life, but death is the death of death and the beginning of an unshadowed life more intense than this present one. This truth, fully accepted, breeds an eagerness to pass the gate—

> As to a hound that mewing waits
> Death opens and shuts to his gates.

188

Death is ineffectual, to end or to tear apart: it shall complete life and establish an endless union.

> Life is a mockery if death
> Hath the least power men say it hath.

But the completion and the union are not of that rich exhilarating kind apprehended by earlier and some more recent writers. It is a union of unbroken sleep, completion in a changeless peace. Death, thus conceived, is much to be desired (though once he reminds himself that "even in the grave thou wilt have thyself"). Whether as a gateway into the unknown (a later image) or, as generally here, an entering upon peace, it puts a term to the troublous wakefulness of life. "A dream my all, the all I ask is sleep." The lure of life is faint, for even beauty deceives:

> All I love
> In beauty cries to me,
> "We but vain shadows
> And reflections be".

Life's saving grace is its fleetingness—"The transient strangeness of the earth"; the beloved but a "flower of a moment in the eternal hour". The restlessness of life oppresses de la Mare as it oppressed Arnold. To us who have lived for years in fear from day to day it seems odd that Arnold should have written from the peace of the Victorians and de la Mare (all the poems just referred to) from those pre-1914 decades upon which we (and de la Mare not least) so wistfully look back. But reasonably or not, the restless, changing quality of life oppresses the poet, making life a burden, a riddle, "an endless war 'twixt contrarieties"; hence peace must mean changelessness—

> Where all things transient to the changeless win,
> There waits the peace thy spirit dwelleth in.

And since life is change, changelessness is death, and —nothing. Nothingness is a positive ideal to de la Mare. That strange great poem, *The Tryst* (a), shows "mortal longingness" seeking for sleep, rest, silence; and it concludes,

> Somewhere there Nothing is, and there lost Man
> Shall win what changeless vague of peace he can.

Just once, in that expression of subjective idealism, *Evening*, the dream is invested with a suggestion of dubiety: space and time have "their only being in what has place at pin-point moment in the mind"; we nod, and the instant-point fades, and space-time with it. What, asks the poet, happens "at the last slumber's nod"?

Time, transience, death, changelessness, nothing: these ideas float and intermingle through de la Mare's poetry, suggesting a sort of lyric space-time continuum. The exiled Adam is to re-welcome Eve to "heaven's nothingness". The titmouse flies away into "time's enormous nought". The Knight and his horse stand in unimaginable loneliness upon a "steep of time". Past and present fade into the eternal now in

All That's Past, and the rose roves back through her wild centuries.

Of death in its secondary aspect, as something which tears our loved ones out of our hearts, de la Mare has two things to say. "Recollection in tranquillity" furnishes the great conception of *When the Rose is Faded:* dead beauty lives in memory without the bond of life:

'Tis the immortal thought
Whose passion still
Makes of the changing
The unchangeable.

O, thus thy beauty,
Loveliest on earth to me,
Dark with no sorrow, shines
And burns, with Thee.

But this serene and passionate vision gives place to the agonized bereavement of the tragic love-poems, where we see the inadequacy of the most vivid sense of "the immortal thought" to assuage personal loss. Even if death be "accepted" as the completion of life, as an experience no less significant than birth, as something that gives changeless form to an immortal thought, still there must be torture to see death's scythe swinging here, slashing there, ruthlessly, disastrously, stupidly.

We can trace three phases of the main theme. In *The Listeners* and *Motley* death was a thing of many moods, nearly all in their way beautiful. It was a beloved ghost that hovered near, a soul that wandered, a spirit flying by; it was a sleep, a longed-for rest; it was the changeless peace of nothingness; it was a child's vision, puzzling but friendly; it was a sense of irreparable loss, agonizingly painful but agonizingly sweet. The touch of flesh—hand exploring face—reminds "how much death does, and yet can do no more." Later there entered fear. Death appeared as a quiet enemy walking pace for pace, as one who holds ajar a wicket out into the dark that swings but one way, or as a viewless wraith who waits on the other side of a bridge leading into the unknown. "Death with a stony gaze is ever near". If death is sometimes strange and fair, a voice from a far-off happy country, a siren that lures, it is because there is no peace on earth—because we are but "waiting to die". And now, in that sweet book *The Burning-Glass*, the poet can turn on death an eye that is almost humorous, certainly tolerant. If he points his finger at it and calls it "that bleak gulf", next moment it is just poet's bedtime, the shutting down of evening—though indeed he "scarce can bear it when the Sun goes in". He fears it will hold no least phantom of the beloved, yet it appears as a long home for "the lost one within me", a sleep none can trouble; a room dark indeed and narrow, "but no grief, no repining will deepen its gloom". If the picture of death's realm given in *Outer Darkness* is macabre it is light-hearted. *A Recluse* is "reconciled to die, as he had lived, a child". And acceptance becomes passionate when the spent wanderer is called home by that vision of a "starry face bound in grave strands of hair".

Even so we must not let death have the last word.

192

Truth and de la Mare

Truth so exalted and so profound as to partake of the nature of direct intuition is contained in three poems whose purpose is to pass a benediction on life out of a heart full of love and deep happiness. The poems stand together at the close of the *Motley* volume. *For All the Grief* is a prayer that calls down upon the lonely, the sad and the dying the blessing of beauty and silence and loving-kindness. *The Scribe* reflects de la Mare's rare theism. The tale of the "lovely things" God's hand has made is too long to be told. And if the record could be completed it would not include God who made the lovely things and man who exists to make the record of them. Here we see, not for the first time, with what bland and royal ease the poets anticipate the laboriously achieved conclusions of the scientists. In *The Mysterious Universe* Sir James Jeans finds that nature is the medium of contact between human consciousness and God, each existing outside the space-time continuum. What is this but?—

> Still would remain
> My wit to try—
> My worn reeds broken,
> The dark tarn dry,
> All words forgotten—
> Thou, Lord, and I.

The third poem, *Fare Well*, is addressed to that other divinity of Beauty. It contains a perfect definition of de la Mare—

> How will fare the world *whose wonder*
> *Was the very proof of me?*

It prays that loved and loving faces, and the Traveller's Joy on the rusting harvest hedge-row, may please other men and happy children. It proposes the marvellous precept

> Look thy last on all things lovely
> Every hour.

It seems to me that de la Mare must have walked very near to the bitterness of death to have discovered that receipt for wringing the last drop of anguished joy from life. The poem concludes by putting this precept into a form more within the compass of the ordinary mortal—unblessed or uncursed by superhuman experience:

> Let no night
> Seal thy sense in deathly slumber
> Till to delight
> Thou hast paid thy utmost blessing,
> Since that all things thou wouldst praise
> Beauty took from those who loved them
> In other days.

Here are banners of unchallengeable truth, flaunting, moreover, those attractive colours of which truth to-day is so often deprived.

Our wanderings among the contributions de la Mare has made to an understanding of life have served, if for little else, to show him not of the tribe of Berkeley and Hume, Alexander and Joad. His poems—when they are not star-holes into eternity—are, like Hardy's novels, "impressions of life", and a poet's impressions are as interesting, and maybe as valuable, as the cerebrations of a philosopher.

> We are such stuff
> As dreams are made on;
>
> All our yesterdays have lighted fools
> The way to dusty death.

These are no reasoned schemes; and they stand like the stars while a hundred schemes, reasoned never so wisely, give place to a hundred others that will be abandoned in their turn. Try to find a "moral" in music, as Browning does, and you are condemned not only by those who find a different moral but by the musicians, who will have no moral at all. Better again take Shakespeare's way:

> The man that hath no music in his soul. . . .
> Is fit for treasons, stratagems and spoils.
>
> It gives a very echo to the seat
> Where love is throned.

Poetry is to be a criticism of life, but life is the work of a master, and demands the critical method appropriate to a masterpiece—that the trained and sensitive mind should be exposed to it, and the resulting "impression" printed off as a glimpse of one of the infinite facets of truth.

I HAVE accepted Arnold's admirable definition of literature as a criticism of life, but in truth the poetry of Walter de la Mare is not essentially either a criticism of life or (as some think it) an escape from life. It will fulfil both these functions for those who require them, but the primary end of de la Mare's poetry is to heighten life. Life is much too good that any but the very unfortunate or the very dull should want to escape from it, but there are times when the pressure, perhaps the preponderance, of its lower constituents creates a sense of insignificance in life itself. At such times a draught, a breath, of de la Mare, even a fleeting memory of one of his poems, effects a miraculous restoration, so that life again is full of meaning and beauty. If the lower levels are your choice, if your interests are "business" and "sport", exalting your ego or overreaching your neighbour, you will have no use for de la Mare; but all the major themes of life he ennobles by making them eternal, part of the world of spirit. It is not altogether a matter of his special insistence on the necessity of magic, but of course it is partly this. He makes us feel in our hearts the strangeness of a phantom world, its stillness answering our cry. Dark hints and intriguing voices come out of the sounds that break the silence of nature, and the silence of a wood or a still house is burdened with meaning. The vaguely, deliciously disturbing atmosphere of quiet places is interpreted for us. Enchantment is ever at hand—ages may fall on you, ages fall from you; you too are

196

haunted by the lutes and forests of Arabia; and if you sit alone the ghost of one who was beautiful beyond all dreams may come knocking. Under de la Mare's spell music is more than a concord of sweet sounds: it has power upon our inmost spirit. His verse instructs our ear to hear a hidden music in the mind, as of the cuckoo tolling to and fro in green and secret ways.

The magic of looking imaginatively forward, inward, outward, is hardly greater than that which comes of looking back. To the reader of de la Mare memory grows more subtle. It has a strange and lovely power of preserving trifles and happy moments —flies in amber. It is as dewfall in the mind, waking to life isles of the lost Hesperides. It acts creatively upon the present: the now may fade out, and our hearts stand still in the hush of an age gone by; more, we see every instant steeped in the past, and as wise as Solomon. The bowers of memory are sweet to the tune of Once . . . once upon a time. Especially does de la Mare make marvellous for us the world—half memory and half imagination—of sleep and dream. Sleep, with still and lovely face and clear grave eyes as of a long-lost peace, befriends the soul. We pass down the quiet steeps of dreamland, out of the dream of wake into the dream of sleep, into the house where Silence and Dark dwell together. The secret symbols of dream are more than a solace to the troubled mind: they bridge a gulf, and are a means by which humanity may be at one with Nature's mystery.

The themes which excite the intensity of de la Mare's passion, and which in consequence he makes

more passionately intense for us, are all spiritual. Of
love he speaks as of something special and strange, so
that those to whom he has spoken can never let love
sink into commonplace, but must always see it as godlike, breathing a speechless grace; an inexpressible
union of the spirits of man and woman, a "selfless
solitude in one another's arms". Though it should be
but a haunted house that love comes to share, it is
roofed by the starry arch of the skies and shaken by
the sea's thunder. There is always a ghostly accom-
paniment beside which love's reality becomes almost
unimportant—"O ghost, draw nearer, let thy shadowy hair. . . ." It is lovers' delight to seek some close-
hid shadow where two might happy be—a lost mer-
maiden's grot beyond the rumour of Paradise. The
memory of love is to be kept unperplexed in the
heart; the ghost of lost love, though but the flower of a
moment in the eternal hour, shall still the sorrowing
of the dream of life, for, when life's troubled bubble
breaks,

> All time's delight
> Hath she for narrow bed.

He illuminates childhood, because he is illuminated by the echoing memories of its eternal hours.
Childhood is a crystal, and he who can hold it in his
hand shall see deep into the heart of things, and may
hope to die as he has lived—a child. The mature mind
should still be a garden for children; but there is an
Eden of the heart, a fellowship with innocence, that
only children know.

Life itself, the all that we have, the grand sum of

our being and knowing from birth to death, is marvellously transmuted, transfigured, heightened in
value and beauty by the poetry of Walter de la Mare,
as he listens in his heart for what is beyond the range
of human speech. He, more than most poets, keeps
alive an endless wonder in the visible world suspended
between God and man. For appearance is not altogether illusion: it is an illusory aspect of reality, and
so has a breathless wonder of its own. The "realness"
of life is tested by its wonder. It is in the mystery of
beauty that the chief "value" of beauty lies, beauty
with its changeless vision of a starry face. Life is an
unbroken pilgrimage: the poet is his own Traveller,
his being laved in the flow of experience. Life is a
sacrament, wherein miraculous wine and bread are
proffered to our lips; in peace or strife life is still a
wondrous thing. Beautiful itself, it is a mirror reflect-
ing the greater beauty of spirit, of love. Its most
familiar things are both loveliest and strangest. Life is
indeed transient, but so varied and wonderful as to
wear at least a semblance of infinity.

Of happiness, life's profoundest truth, de la Mare
has little explicitly to say, and that little comes late, but
when it comes, it comes with an emphasis born of
knowledge, a finality that gives it special force. It has
always been there, silent, in the poetry, for all creation,
whether of God or of genius, is in essence happy. But
his ultimate word is that love, beauty and happiness
are the sacred triunity of life. Life so conceived, so
lived, is hard to abandon, and to the poet with his
intense life doubly so. Loving the light, he is im-
patient of the advancing dark—for to him it is Good

199

night, not "in some other clime" Good morning—
but he breathes a final *Benedicite* over beauty's golden
head, a last prayer of homage and praise, love and
gratitude for the supreme gift of life. . . .

> And then the night-tide of the all-welcoming grave
> For those who weary, and a respite crave:
> Inn at the cross-roads, and the traveller's rest. . . .

V

A BIBLIOGRAPHY
OF DE LA MARE'S POETRY

(The place of publication is London unless otherwise indicated).

Songs of Childhood . . . (under the pseudonym of Walter Ramal). . . . Longmans, 1902.
Poems. . . . Murray, 1906.
A Child's Day, a book of rhymes to pictures by Carine and Will Cadby. . . . Constable, 1912.
The Listeners and other poems. . . . Constable, 1912.
Peacock Pie. . . . Constable, 1913.
The Sunken Garden and other poems. . . . C. W. Beaumont, 1917.
Motley and other poems. . . . Constable, 1918.
Flora, a book of drawings by Pamela Bianco with illustrative poems by Walter de la Mare. . . . Heinemann, 1919.
Poems 1901 *to* 1918, 2 volumes. . . . Constable, 1920.
Crossings, a play (prose but with songs). . . . Beaumont Press, 1921.
The Veil and other poems. . . . Constable, 1921.
Down-adown-Derry, a book of fairy poems. . . . Constable, 1922.
Thus Her Tale. . . . Porpoise Press, 1923.
A Ballad of Christmas. . . . Selwyn and Blount, 1924.
Before Dawn. . . . Selwyn and Blount, 1924.
Ding, Dong, Bell (prose but with verses). . . . Selwyn and Blount, 1924.
Stuff and Nonsense and so on. . . . Constable, 1927.
Alone. . . . Faber and Gwyer, 1927.

A Bibliography of de la Mare's Poetry

Self to Self. . . . Faber and Gwyer, 1928.
A Snowdrop. . . . Faber and Faber, 1929.
News. . . . Faber and Faber, 1930.
Poems for Children. . . . Constable, 1930.
To Lucy. . . . Faber and Faber, 1931.
The Fleeting and other poems. . . . Constable, 1933.
Poems 1919 to 1934. . . . Constable, 1935.
This Year, Next Year. . . . Faber and Faber, 1937.
Memory and other poems. . . . Constable, 1938.
In a Library (with a poem by Arthur Rogers) . . .
    privately printed, Newcastle-on-Tyne, 1938.
Haunted. . . . Linden Press, 1939.
Bells and Grass, a book of rhymes. . . . Faber and
    Faber, 1941.
Collected Poems. . . . Faber and Faber, 1942.
Collected Rhymes and Verses. . . . Faber and Faber,
    1944.
The Burning-Glass and other poems. . . . Faber and
    Faber, 1945.
The Traveller. . . . Faber and Faber, 1946.
Rhymes and Verses (collected poems for children). . . .
    Henry Holt, New York, 1947.

INDEX

INDEX

205

Index

Index

II. POETRY VOLUMES

III PROSE VOLUMES AND COLLECTIONS

IV. TOPICS

(topics comprised under chapterheadings are generally
not included here)

Index

V. NAMES

Index